The Surrey Village Book

October 1990

To Phil —

    Just so that you don't
forget where to come
back to!

Tony, Janet, Christopher and Nicholas

THE VILLAGES OF BRITAIN SERIES

Other counties in this series include:

*Published in conjunction with County Federations
of Women's Institutes

The Surrey Village Book

GRAHAM COLLYER

with illustrations by Christopher Howkins

COUNTRYSIDE BOOKS

NEWBURY

First Published 1984
© Graham Collyer 1984
Revised and Reprinted 1986, 1988
Reprinted 1990
All rights reserved. No reproduction
permitted without the
prior permission of the publishers:
Countryside Books
3, Catherine Road, Newbury, Berkshire.

ISBN 0 905392 32 9

Designed by Mon Mohan.

Cover photograph of Abinger Hammer by H.H. Dennis ARPS FRSA

Produced through MRM Associates Ltd., Reading

Printed in Great Britain by
J.W. Arrowsmith Ltd., Bristol.

To Ann, David, Laurie and Esther

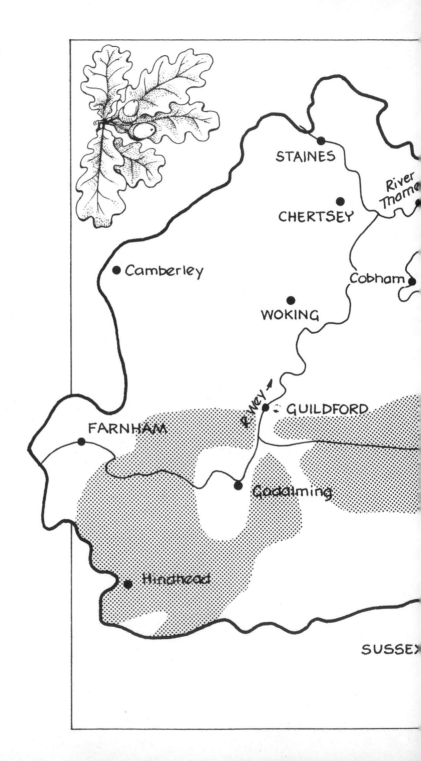

County of SURREY

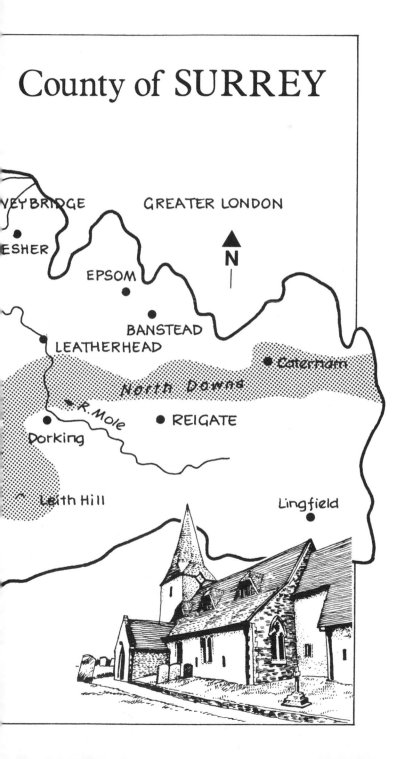

WEYBRIDGE

GREATER LONDON

ESHER

N

EPSOM

BANSTEAD

LEATHERHEAD

Caterham

North Downs

R.Mole

REIGATE

Dorking

Leith Hill

Lingfield

Country path in Wey Meadows

Introduction

It was William Cobbett who wrote in October 1825: 'Those that travel on turnpike roads know nothing of England.' Cobbett was a Surrey man, born in a farmhouse in Farnham. I, too, am a Surrey man, born in a wartime nursing home in Rowledge, no more than three miles from Cobbett's birthplace. My family's roots are deep in the sandy soil of south-west Surrey; the spelling of my surname is the Surrey form.

My years as a junior reporter on the *Farnham Herald* took me to every village and hamlet in south-west Surrey. I was encouraged to get to know the places and the people by my editor, the late Mr L.T. Pope, who was, I think, the greatest influence on my chosen career. He also fostered my great love of village cricket and this is reflected in many of the passages on the pages which follow.

Now, as editor of the *Surrey Advertiser*, I am based in the county town of Guildford and surrounded by villages, some still quite rural, many with a more modern appearance and home to people who earn their living in the capital. Cobbett would, I suppose, be shocked at Surrey in the latter part of the 20th century. His *Rural Rides* can be, and indeed have been, retraced, but so much of what the great man saw has disappeared. Those who love the county now must be on their guard to protect their heritage from over-zealous planners and despoilers of the countryside.

Cobbett's turnpikes have been replaced by fast trunk roads and even faster motorways, both of which criss-cross Surrey, but away from these are the lanes and the byways along which the best of any county can be seen. Surrey's network of lanes, with their high hedgerows and secluded cottages, are a delight. I did not know how much I loved the county until I returned to it after six years abroad, and that was when I set out to discover more.

I hope by this book to show how enjoyable such journeys of discovery can be.

Graham Collyer
Hindhead
1990

Abinger

Lutyens was at work in Abinger to the south of the A25. He built Goddards in 1898-9 as a hostel for young women and then added two rooms a decade later when the property was converted to a private house. The great Surrey architect also converted a 17th century cottage into a post office in 1899 but this is once more a cottage.

There is a war memorial by Lutyens in the churchyard of St James which is claimed to be the second highest old parish church in the county. It was bombed during the war, restored in 1950 and then again 14 years later after a fire. Near the church, and almost lost in the passing years, is St James' Well which was built by William John Evelyn, Lord of the Manor of Abinger, and declared open to the parishioners on August 11, 1893. The now demolished Abinger Hall was where Darwin used Roman mosaic floors in a field to observe the earth worm.

The hamlet of Sutton to the west has two old farm houses; one, Sutton Place Farm, which was built around 1700, the other, Fulvens, is earlier and stated by Pevsner and Nairn to be one of the best farms in the county. The residents of Sutton have been plagued by lorries in the narrow lanes, caused it seems by the much larger Sutton, once of the county but now in Greater London, continuing to have Surrey as part of its address. This hamlet is a far cry from any London borough.

Abinger Hammer

Everyone who travels the A25 through Abinger Hammer knows of the village clock. It stands proudly over the winding street and on the hour Jack the Hammer strikes out the time on his anvil. The clock, given in memory of the first Lord Farrer of Abinger Hall who died in 1899, reminds us of the importance this area played in the Surrey iron industry of long ago. The Tillingbourne stream was dammed at various points to create the hammer ponds the iron masters required to carry out their craft, and these have now been utilised by watercress growers who find the chalk beds ideal for their product.

Abinger Hammer is a popular spot in summer but the narrowness of the main road is a source of irritation. Cricket is played beside the road on land given as a memorial to the men from the village who died in the Great War. North of the A25 Hackhurst Downs rise to 733ft and there is a granite pillar marking the spot where Samuel Wilberforce, who was Bishop of Winchester and son of the abolitionist William Wilberforce, was thrown from his horse and fatally injured in 1873.

The people of Abinger Hammer run their own village school, recognised by the Charity Commissioners after the county council withdrew its support. The school is on a rise behind the famous clock and first opened for business in 1873, the gift of Thomas Henry Farrer and his wife. Five years later Farrer handed over the reins to a local committee, and alterations followed in 1881 and 1893 before the county took control in 1906. Fortunately, the county did not become the owner of the building and this proved to be vital when the decision came a few years back from the education committee to close the school.

Albury

Magisterial orders in 1784 began a process that was not completed until well into the 19th century. The result was that the present village of Albury was established, with the great architect, Pugin, influencing the style. His delightful chimneys are still in evidence today. The village was formerly in Albury Park and the move was completed when the estate was bought by Henry Drummond in 1819. In 1840 Drummond built the Catholic Apostolic Church for the Irvingite Sect and it stands as a striking landmark near the junction of the A25 and the A248 into the village.

Close to that junction is the Silent Pool, more properly Shireborne Pond, which is a popular spot with walkers and the location for Martin Tupper's novel, *Stephan Langton*. Tupper, who encouraged African literature and was an inventor, lived at Albury Park from 1850 to 1860.

Cobbett and, earlier, Evelyn concerned themselves with Albury. Cobbett, on one of his rides, indulged in what he called a 'pretty

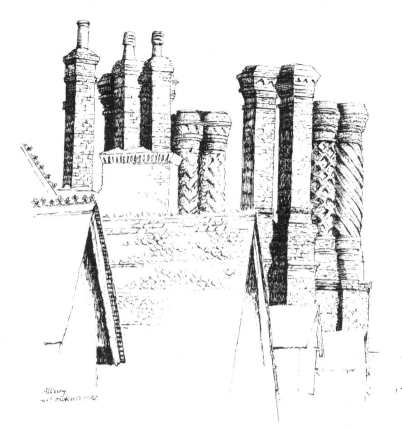

bare-faced' move by entering Albury Park and asking for Mr Drummond's permission to continue on through in order to reach Shere. The request was not only granted, said Cobbett, but the 'prettiest' gardens in England were opened up for his perusal. Evelyn was credited with making the gardens.

A mill and a church in Albury were recorded in the Domesday survey, but there have been several mills in the district, one of which was burned down on November 13, 1830. According to the *Surrey Advertiser*, in an historical note, one 'Doggy' Warner was the culprit. He also shot at the miller, James Franks, and after a trial at Guildford Assizes went to the gallows. Almost 250 years earlier there was another hanging being talked about in the village although as was the custom in Elizabethan times the punishment did not fit the crime. Robert Wintershull, gent., of Albury, was hanged for burglary. He was found guilty of entering the house of a fellow villager, William Otway, and stealing a coverlet and three pillowbars valued at £3.

Alfold

There are so many pretty approaches to Surrey's parish churches but the path up to St Nicholas at Alfold surely cannot be bettered for simplicity and beauty. Everything is in scale as one looks towards the church from the village square. Old cottages on the right look out on to the stocks and across the fields to Sussex. The cobbled path takes the visitor to the churchyard gate and beyond to the little church, which dates from 1100, and a yew which is as old as any in the county. It was Eric Parker who noticed that the yews at Alfold, Dunsfold and Hambledon stand *'almost in a mathematically straight line'*.

Alfold, which has the Sussex border at its doorstep, had no made-up roads until 1809 and was as rural a place as one could find. And yet more than 200 years before that it was a bustling glass-making centre. A slab of Sussex marble in the churchyard is said to mark the grave of Jean Carré who was one of the last French glass-makers in the Fold country. The industry was carried out in Sidney Wood and Carré had been granted a licence five years before his death in 1572 to make glass similar to that in his own country.

The village was on a smuggling route from the Sussex coast, and tobacco and brandy were left at Alfold farm houses at the dead of night, in return for food.

Artington

The trees have grown so tall on St Catherine's hill that the ruins of a chapel on its top are no longer easily discernible to the passer-by. Which is a shame because those old sandstones have been a landmark for centuries. St Catherine's Chapel dates from 1317 but was undoubtedly built on the site of a much earlier place of worship.

Folk lore has it that two sisters were responsible for building the chapel, and that of St Martha a few miles away. It was said they threw a hammer back and forth to each other. The inside measurement is 45ft 6in by 20ft 6in, and it had five doors which is curious in so small a building. Two of them were let into windows so it seems likely that ladders were used to allow access to upstairs accommodation.

The ruins are close to what has become popularly known as the Pilgrims Way – a footpath that has been used for centuries by all manner of people. The path crossed the river into Shalford meadows where there was a large annual fair in medieval times. The crossing was either by punt or plank, and it is not so long ago that a boat was used to carry pedestrians. Now there is a modern footbridge.

The old coaching route to Portsmouth runs below St Catherine's and the railway line enters a tunnel beneath it. The community of Artington has changed little in spite of the arrival of the County Police Headquarters and the law college.

Ash 🌿

The parish is in the Borough of Guildford but is always associated with Aldershot because of its close proximity to the Hampshire town. The county boundary is all that separates the two. Ribbon development between Ash and Ash Vale has taken away any last vestige of village appearance. Ash Green to the south remains pleasantly rural. Nearby, Wyke was the scene of a fruitless search for oil earlier in the decade.

Old Ash can still be seen between the church of St Peter and the Greyhound public house. A cottage close to the church used to be the Harts Horn Inn where, it is said, Dick Turpin was a visitor. In truth, if there is such a thing in this instance, another highwayman, Jeremiah Abershaw, could have been the robber in question for it was he who appeared at nearby Guildford Sessions on Wednesday, August 8, 1792. Abershaw, a 22-year-old shoemaker, had been accused the previous day of felonious assault on the King's Highway in the County of Essex. He was charged with stealing a gold watch and other things. Abershaw, whose real name was said to be Avershaw, was tried at Croydon on July 30, 1795, and hanged on Kennington Common.

Ashford 🌿

Ashford Common, where cavalry regiments were reviewed by the King in the early 1800s, was probably the traditional meeting place of the Spelthorne Hundred when the area was in Middlesex. Now there is very little open space left in Spelthorne, the borough that was created in 1974 and which added a sizeable north-west area to Surrey.

Spelthorne is a borough which is administered from Staines and overflown in no uncertain manner by the jets which use London Airport at Heathrow. Much of its area is covered by water for it is a borough of reservoirs, some purpose built, others formed from old gravel workings.

Ashford, which was known as Exeford in Domesday times, has always been associated with Staines and became part of an urban district in 1930. St Matthew's church was built about 1860 and part of the cost was defrayed by the Welsh School which came to the village at the time the church was being constructed. Now St David's Girls School it received in exchange for putting up some of the cost 212 seats in perpetuity. In the churchyard is a floor slab which marks the site of a Norman chancel.

Ashtead ✺

Samuel Pepys wrote about Ashtead in his diaries, about the 'little hole' he could not stand upright in where he stayed overnight. On July 25, 1663, he wrote: 'When we come there (Epsom) we could hear of no lodging, the town so full; but, which was better, I went towards Ashtead, my old place of pleasure, and there by direction of one goodman Arthur, whom we met on the way, we went to Farmer Page's, at which direction he and I made good sport, and there we got a lodging in a little hole we could not stand upright in, but rather than go further to look we staid there, and while supper was getting ready I took him to walk up and down behind my cozen Pepys' house that was, which I find comes little short of what I took it to be when I was a little boy.' The year before Pepys had written: 'I eat, among other fruit, much mulberrys, a thing I have not eat of these many years, since I used to be at Ashtead, at my cozen Pepys.'

Ashtead is on the main road between Leatherhead and Epsom and has some nice touches still. It was not until the 1930s that it was developed; previously it had been an agricultural village. Ashtead woods and common are beloved of walkers and riders and Ashtead Park has some open space. A Romano-British villa was found on the common in 1926 and contained 12 rooms and a four-room bath annexe. There was a large bath house some distance away, and some of the tiles which were decorated with hunting scenes were incorporated in the church of St. Giles. The villa was occupied between the first and third centuries as revealed by coins and pottery found at the site.

Badshot Lea ❧

In spite of the close proximity of both Farnham and Aldershot, Badshot Lea has survived to retain its own identity. Old kilns and oast houses are a reminder of the hop fields which once covered the land in this part of the county. Badshot Lea is a village which is interested in its history, and an exhibition in 1984 gave a vivid picture of life through the ages. It also explained the legend of the Badshot Lea 'docks' which has fascinated people for decades. How could a small village, situated miles from the sea or a navigable waterway, have a docks? The answer, apparently, was to be found in the terrible flooding the village endured in times gone by. The road near the Aldershot boundary became a pond and, at the turn of the century, the area was nicknamed the 'docks'.

For 34 years William Rankine was the headmaster of the village school. He was a Scot who came to Farnham with his parents and became a leading authority on the Mesolithic period. His archaeological work in the district has been much valued, but it was not until 1983 that his discoveries were seen by the public when an exhibition was mounted in Farnham Museum. Until then the artefacts had lain in cardboard boxes gathering dust since the former teacher's death in 1962.

Bagshot ❧

Bagshot Heath was 'not only good for little but good for nothing' said Defoe. The heath was the haunt of highwaymen and other undesirables, but it was the source of fuel. Turf sold for 2s 6d a load. However, improved husbandry in the 18th century brought about a change. In 1754 the Rev. Edward Cooper said he thought the soil was too poor to bear wheat, but then someone introduced chalk – brought by wagon from the Hog's Back at Seale – and clover seeds, and the condition of the soil was enhanced.

Extensive nurseries were established and today Bagshot is famous for its rhododendrons and azaleas. Gardeners come from far and wide to buy from the nurseries alongside the A30 which in recent years has given up much of its through traffic to the M3.

Bagshot became an important staging post in the days of the coach and four, and in busy times as many as 30 changes of horses were made in the village. There were 14 inns to cater for the visitors. Perhaps there are not that many now, but those that remain do a good trade. The Jolly Farmer, it is said, used to be known as the Golden Farmer because of a notorious highwayman on the heath who touched nothing but gold and a farmer at nearby Frimley who paid his debts only in gold. The two were at last recognised as the same person, and the inn is close to the spot where the villain was hanged.

St Anne's Church has memorials to members of the Royal Family given by the Duke of Connaught who lived at Bagshot Park.

Betchworth

Travellers by train on the picturesque line between Guildford and Redhill pass through Betchworth station but see nothing of the village, for it is to the south beyond the A25 road. It is a quiet place through which the river Mole meanders. The Domesday church has been replaced by one that retains Norman traces, and whose original tower was moved in the middle of the last century because it was found to be unsafe.

Among the memorials in St Michael's is one to Sir Benjamin Brodie who was a surgeon to Queen Victoria. He was one of three Betchworth doctors who cared for the Royal Family: the others being Thomas Morsted who was surgeon to Henry V and was at Agincourt, and Dyce Duckworth earlier this century.

The entrance to the churchyard is by way of a narrow path bordered by cottages opposite which is the Dolphin Inn where the landlord brewed his own ale until 1926. Across the lane which leads to Leigh are 16th century cottages said to be genuine and untouched by any fake or restoration.

There was a castle at Betchworth on a knoll above the river but it is long since gone. It was probably of 14th century origin and is likely not to have seen action. During Queen Anne's reign it fell into disrepair, was dismantled and a private house built on the spot. But this too is gone.

Records show that there was a case of witchcraft in Betchworth in the 16th century, and that the defendant, George Brockham, a clerk, was tried in his absence at Southwark Assizes in March 1576 and found not guilty. His alleged crime? That he did bewitch to death a bull valued at £2! Other villagers were not so fortunate. Richard Hole, a bricklayer, appeared at Croydon Assizes in 1580 and was sentenced to hang for burglary of a house at Horley and the theft of cloth valued at £3 10s. And Michael Lamb, a yeoman, confessed to highway robbery in 1581 and 1582 and was hanged.

Bisley

When the National Rifle Association transferred from Wimbledon to the wild common near Woking, Bisley came to the notice of the world. Now, for a fortnight in July this unlikely place plays host to top marksmen from all parts of the globe. Fame does not appear to have rubbed off on the village which goes about its daily business with barely a second thought for the crack shots out on the common.

In days gone by the village was centred more on the ancient church of St John the Baptist, a few hundred yards from which a holy well was, by tradition, the place where children were baptised. The water in the spring was said to be colder in summer and warmer in winter.

Gen. Charles Gordon of Khartoum is remembered at nearby West End where the Gordon Boys' Home was established at a cost of £24,000 in 1885. Gordon had been killed in that year during a revolt in Sudan.

Blackheath

Tucked away behind Chilworth and Wonersh, Blackheath is a delightful little place whose pub, The Villagers, attracts many visitors on a warm summer evening. They come, too, to watch cricket on an attractive ground near the pub. Blackheath Cricket Club is well into its second century. The church of St Martin was completed in 1895 to the design of a Cheshire-born architect, Charles Harrison Townsend, whose most influential work is to be found in London. He designed several other buildings in Blackheath, including Cobbins for himself but in which he is not believed to have lived. Blatchfeld was built for Sir William Roberts-Austen, chemist and assayer and at one time deputy master of the Royal Mint, who, as a lay preacher, held services in a cottage which was incorporated in St Martin's church and is now the vestry.

Bletchingley 🦢

The wide A25 cuts a swathe through this charming village which once had a castle and returned two MPs to Westminster. Bletchingley today is much visited. Its tile-hung cottages along the High Street, and the Whyte Harte Inn ('AD 1388') overlooking the 11th century St Mary's church are the favourite subjects of photographers.

The castle was first mentioned in 1160 and was said to be one of four in the county. Its life, though, was short as it was destroyed in 1264 during Henry III's war with Simon de Montfort. Men from the garrison were despatched to Canterbury to guard Thomas a'Becket shortly before his martyrdom. Castle Hill and Castle Street at the west end of the village are reminders of the long gone past.

Cobbett's description of the place as a 'vile rotten borough' came towards the end of Bletchingley's political life. It was electing two Members of Parliament in spite of the fact that the number of voters could almost be counted on the fingers of one's hands. It became a borough in the early 13th century but never had a royal charter. The first MPs were returned in 1285 and the last in 1829 – prior to the 1832 Reform Act. Two of the incumbents in the final years of representation in Bletchingley were William Lamb, later Lord Melbourne, PM from 1834-41 and a mentor of young Queen Victoria, and Lord Palmerston.

That Bletchingley has known great times is illustrated in the history of the palace which the Duke of Buckingham built there early in the 16th century. The Duke and Sir Nicholas Carew, who suc-

ceeded him, were executed, and the manor came into the hands of Anne of Cleves whose head was spared in spite of her divorce from Henry VIII.

Bookhams

The National Trust property, Polesden Lacey at Great Bookham, was where the Duke and Duchess of York spent their honeymoon. Later, of course, they became the King and Queen of England – George VI and Elizabeth. Polesden Lacey was given to the Trust in 1942 by the Hon. Mrs Ronald Greville as a memorial to her father, the Rt. Hon. William McEwan. The gift comprised the house, the gardens, an estate of 1000 acres, pictures and other works of art. The present house was begun in 1824, eight years after the original mansion had been pulled down.

Great Bookham's church of St Nicholas is Norman on a Saxon site of worship, and has welcomed many distinguished people into its congregation, not least the future king and queen. An east window is a memorial to Lord Raglan who lost his life at Sebastopol 40 years after losing an arm at the Battle of Waterloo. The rector from 1769 until his death in 1820 was Jane Austen's godfather, the Rev. Samuel Cooke.

The Surrey novelist Fanny Burney lived at a cottage called Fairfield (now The Hermitage) for four years after her marriage to General d'Arblay at Mickleham in 1793. The couple had a child and told the world they were blissfully happy on £125 a year. Fanny wrote *Camilla* while at Great Bookham. Elizabeth Barrett was said to have resided at the Old Rectory; her father rented the property in 1846 in an attempt to get his daughter, who spent much of her time on her back after an injury during childhood, to forget Robert Browning. But as the two poets married in that year and spent much time abroad, it seems that Elizabeth was at Bookham infrequently if at all.

Thomas Briggs, a butcher of Great Bookham, was hanged in January 1594 after being found guilty of breaking into a property at Newdigate and stealing two oxen valued at £8.

Little Bookham has a church, whose dedication is unknown, which has some 12th century work. The church is thought to contain four periods of medieval architecture. The original building comprised only a nave and a south aisle was added around 1160. The north and west walls of this building are still in existence. A tithe barn near the church is probably 15th century and there are a number of 16th century buildings in the village, including the Windsor Castle public house.

The Bourne

There are three Bournes — Upper, Middle and Lower — which come together as The Bourne, and the prefix is important to local people. The area lies either side of the Bourne stream which starts its life as a Hampshire outflow from Lodge Pond in Alice Holt Forest, then runs along the floor of The Bourne before entering the Wey at Moor Park. It has a short life but the stream has given its name to a beautiful locality and a very fine descriptive writer. George Sturt, wheelwright and countryman, used George Bourne as his *nom de plume,* and anyone who reads his books and knows The Bourne can identify the area of a century ago. Sturt lived in Vine Cottage on Vicarage Hill — still a pine-wooded slope down which the lane falls to cross the stream and run beside a pleasant pub called the Spotted Cow.

This is also the district of Cobbett's boyhood. He received his education here, he said, on a sandhill where, with two of his brothers, he played. 'It is impossible to say how much I owe to that sandhill'.

Cobbett's sandhills are still there, now heavily wooded and built upon; but it is not too difficult to imagine them as they were 200 years ago.

The Bourne's hub is the crossroads at Lower Bourne where village shops enjoy a lively trade. The busy A287 sweeps down Gravel Hill from Farnham, leaving the parish church of St Thomas-on-the-Bourne at the top, and departs for the heaths of Frensham over Gong Hill.

One of the pubs on the main road is the Cricketers which serves as a reminder that the summer game is very important to the village. The ground in Old Frensham Road has seen many a stirring game going back to the days of George Sturt's chairmanship. In Upper Bourne are two hostelries renowned for their sporting endeavours — the aptly named Bat and Ball and, as befits the area, the Sandrock. They were once in the thick of the hop fields which covered the hillsides south of Farnham. The Bat and Ball was a tally man's office where pickers were given their hard-earned pay, and was transformed into a pub when the pay was augmented by the supply of ale. The Bat and Ball and the Sandrock get together each year for various sporting contests, and a cricket match between their regulars on The Bourne's ground was featured on BBC radio in John Ebdon's series on rural life.

Bramley

Women's cricket, which has still not been accepted in some quarters in spite of the advances made towards sexual equality, had its birth on Gosden Common beside the road into the village from Guildford. There, in 1745, the maids of Bramley played those from Hambledon, near Godalming, and not, as may be supposed, from the Hampshire village of the same name which will forever be associated with the early age of cricket.

Two years later Bramley's men combined with those from Ripley and Thursley to play London, and another 20 years on a village side was thought good enough to face up to Ripley on the latter's famous cricket green .

Bramley has few if any other claims to immortality. It had a station on the Guildford to Brighton railway line which opened in 1865 and closed 100 years later, and there were two mills, one of them at Snowdenham, close to the home of the late Lord Lieutenant of Surrey, Lord Hamilton of Dalzell. Lord Hamilton was the third baron in a line created in 1886, and was related by marriage to the Ricardo family who came to Bramley in Victoria's reign.

Guildford Museum has on display tokens given out at Bramley school. There was a round token each week for attendance, punctuality and conduct, and six could be exchanged for an oval-shaped disc with a value of 6d. At the end of each year the 'money' collected was lodged in the child's savings account. The money was given by Col. Ricardo who lived at Bramley House from 1886 until the 1930s.

Along the A281 are fine examples of old west Surrey cottages at Birtley Green and the hamlet of Grafham whose ecclesiastical district was formed in 1863 out of the civil parishes of Bramley and Dunsfold. The church of St Andrew at Grafham was built in 1861, designed and paid for by Henry Woodyer who lived at Grafham Grange. Woodyer, who died on August 10, 1896, and was buried in the churchyard, also designed St Peter's at Hascombe and was responsible for some interior alterations to Holy Trinity at the top of Guildford's famous High Street. He was the son of Caleb Woodyer, a Guildford surgeon-doctor. His architecture can also be seen in several schools in Surrey, and in churches in Berkshire, Gloucestershire, Gwent, Herefordshire, Hertfordshire, Staffordshire and Yorkshire.

Brockham

The biggest Guy Fawkes bonfire in Surrey is Brockham's claim. The green by Christ Church is taken over by a massive construction on the morning of the great November celebration, and the village is a place to avoid if you wish to get anywhere in a hurry on the night.

In earlier days Brockham green was a venue for cricket and players of the calibre of Dr. W.G. Grace have been known to play there. The home players wore straw hats manufactured by the village rush-chair maker and Eric Parker wrote that when the team went to Mitcham the derisive shout went up: 'Here come the Brockham straw yards.' But the visitors won by an innings to silence the cocky south Londoners.

The village was the home of Captain Morris of the Lifeguards, a 'convivial lyrist', who lived at Brockham Lodge, and died there in 1838 at the age of 93. He was buried at neighbouring Betchworth as Christ Church had not then been built. Brockham became an ecclesiastical parish, separate from St Michael's, Betchworth, in 1848.

In Victorian times there was a Home and Industrial School for the training of orphan girls for domestic services in the village, plus an infant home.

Brook

There is an attractive pub, the Dog and Pheasant, in this hamlet on the road between Milford and Haslemere. Opposite, there is a delightful cricket ground. What more could one ask for? The six-acre ground was a gift to the neighbourhood by the late Viscount Pirrie in 1923, and the hall, which serves as the pavilion and meeting place and which carries the donor's name, was erected in the same year at a cost of £4000.

Next to Brook is Sandhills hamlet on the road out to Witley, and a century ago the artist, Graham Robertson, called it a 'most unsophisticated little village', in 'the real English countryside'. Roberston, who was also a playwright, had moved into the house in which lived Helen Allingham whose paintings of Surrey are a delight to the eye. Mrs Allingham was the daughter of a doctor in

Burton-on-Trent. She was born in 1848 and after her father died in 1862 the family moved to Birmingham where Helen studied art. She went on to the Royal Academy in London as one of the first intake of women students. She married the poet, William Allingham, in 1874 and the following year they moved to Sandhills. For the next 13 years, working in water-colours, she captured many delightful Surrey scenes which are now sold at auction at what the trade calls keen prices. She was a member of the Royal Society of Painters in Water-colours. Mrs Allingham moved back to London in 1888 but returned to Surrey later and died at Haslemere in 1926.

The area attracted other residents of note, including the artist Birket Foster, and the writer George Eliot, who is remembered by a corner in Witley's 16th century White Hart Inn.

There are some beautiful lanes around Brook which can lead the traveller to the northern slopes of Hindhead. One passes through the sleepy hamlet of Bowlhead Green where there are some charming buildings, including a former chapel. Congregationalism came to this tiny corner of Surrey in 1865 when the man who owned the chapel, Isaac Kettle, began his ministry. He also toured the district handing out tracts and books, and held regular Sunday afternoon cottage meetings. When he died in 1906 his will revealed that he had bequeathed the building to a relative and services were brought to an abrupt close.

Brookwood ✑

A hospital and a cemetery make this village near Woking well known over a wide area. The hospital, established in 1867 as an asylum for pauper lunatics, lies to the north of the main railway line; the cemetery is to the south. An Act of Parliament founded the burial ground which opened in 1854. The Necropolis company of London bought 2000 acres of heath land and laid out one-fifth as a cemetery. It had its own railway line with a station in Westminster Road, London, from which a train departed each morning for Brookwood. A crematorium was constructed in 1889.

Buckland ✣

A gruesome legend is still recounted in these parts. Buckland, a small village between Dorking and Reigate, is known now for its picturesque pond and group of buildings beside the A25, but in pre-Victorian times it was some kind of water monster that made people talk.

The 'thing' – ape-like by all accounts – was known as the Buckland Shag and lived near a stone by a stream. An article in the *Gentleman's Magazine* in 1827 opened: 'The road from Reigate to Dorking leads through a lonely lane, of considerable length, into the village of Buckland. In the most obscure part of this lane a little stream of beautifully clear water crosses the way. By the side of this very stream laid a large stone for I know not how many years – perhaps for centuries.'

The apparition used to appear at midnight and in that 19th century piece were two instances of a person or persons coming face to face with the beast. A Buckland man was returning from Reigate market, the worse for wear, when he entered the lane and saw it. He hit out with his stick but made no impression. He sobered up in a flash and, chased by the ghost, set off for his cottage. When at last he reached his door, he collapsed and was helped to his bed where he died a week later. On another occasion a wagon and four horses reached the spot and would go no further even though the stream was only two feet wide and its depth perfectly manageable.

The Church of Our Lady was rebuilt in 1860. Three hundred years earlier the churchyard was the scene of an offence which had its climax in the assizes. Thomas Dalender, gent., of Buckland was indicted for drawing his sword in the churchyard with the intention of assaulting John Alleayne, a yeoman of the village. History neither records whether Alleayne was injured nor the verdict returned against Dalender.

Buckland today has sand and gravel pits, a delightful green and pond, beside which stands an old barn with a turret – and a property called Shagbrook which stands as a reminder to those who know of the legend of the village.

Burpham

This once rural village is being swallowed up by developers. There are huge housing estates and now a superstore where once there were green fields. Years ago Burpham was distant enough from Guildford for town dwellers to walk through Stoke Park to the village, slake their thirst at The Green Man, and return home again. Now, London Road is continuous building although no longer carrying the vast amount of traffic, thanks to the opening of Guildford's second bypass in half a century.

The Green Man has always been the focal point of the village, and will presumably continue to fulfil that role for a long time to come since in 1593 it was the subject of a 1000-year lease and the freehold was claimed a decade or so ago. The pub was rebuilt at the beginning of this century and underwent substantial change in the 1980s. Attached to it is the Paddock Room, a 19th century private house when it was acquired by the brewers in 1930. Nearer Guildford is the Anchor and Horseshoes which became a public house in the 19th century, and probably got the second part of its name because in earlier times there were stables and a blacksmith's forge on or about the site.

Burpham's little church of St Luke was built in 1859 by the Surrey architect Henry Woodyer and renovated as the centenary was celebrated. It stands above the new A3 and once looked out across open country which has all but been consumed by houses and Guildford's first out of town superstore.

Burstow

This village near the Sussex border means only one thing to me: the birthplace of the great 19th century cricketer William Lambert. Known to his contemporaries as the finest batsman of his age, Lambert was born in 1779 and died in 1851. He lived much of his life in nearby Nutfield, where he was a miller and had an involvement in the fuller's earth trade, but was buried in the churchyard of St Bartholomew's at Burstow.

Lambert was the first player to score a century in both innings of a match at the present Lords ground, when playing for Sussex against Epsom – a curious fixture by today's standards. He scored 107 not out in the first innings and 157 in the second, and it was 76 years later that the feat was next achieved, by A.E. Stoddart who made 195 not out and 124 for Middlesex against Nottingham. Lambert's record was in 1817 and that was a year that turned sour for him as he was 'warned off the turf' at Lord's for allegedly not playing his best – 'selling the match' – in England v Nottinghamshire.

So William Lambert, who the previous year had appeared as the author of a manual entitled *'Instructions and Rules for playing the Noble Game of Cricket'* was drummed out. But he continued to play cricket in the country, especially in Surrey, and his last match was recorded as being in 1839.

Burstow does not appear to have a heart. Perhaps it has been ripped out by the jets which fly into and out of nearby Gatwick Airport, or by the M23 which is even closer. The church, though, is in very rural surroundings. It dates from around 1120 and has a wooden tower and shingle spire. One of its incumbents was John Flamsteed, created the first Astronomer Royal by Charles II. He held the living from 1684 until he died in 1719. It is said he was buried in the chancel. While at Burstow he and Sir Isaac Newton worked on and disputed astronomical subjects. As Eric Parker observed, it was quite an achievement to be made Astronomer Royal when Newton was alive.

Busbridge

How many of the thousands of visitors who annually walk through the glades and groves of Winkworth Arboretum between Busbridge and Hascombe know how such a beautiful and tranquil spot came to be there? The National Trust owns it but the majority of its 100 acres was the creation of one man who, when he bought the then steep hillside covered in hazel scrub and coppice, knew nothing about gardening.

It was in 1938 that Dr Wilfrid Fox, senior consultant at St George's Hospital in London and the outstanding dermatologist of his age, bought Winkworth Farm. He had no interest in gardening but was prepared to learn; he was a man who achieved many things in his life. Soon he founded the Roads Beautifying Association; born out of his despair at seeing daily the barren roadside along the new Kingston bypass.

When the doctor went to Austria on holiday in 1938 land adjoining his home became available for purchase. Telegrams went back and forth and the scrubby hillside was bought. The messages, it was said, attracted the interest of the Germans who thought they were in code. Dr Fox returned from the Continent and with unbridled energy set about transforming the landscape. He did the digging himself, with the help of a retired woodman and occasional parties of friends. Tree planting began with a maple grove for autumn colouring and an azalea glade based on a garden beside Dr Fox's beloved Lake Como.

In 1952 the 60 acres were given to the National Trust who five years later bought an adjoining 35 acres. At the foot of the wooded hillside is a lake and beyond, in a valley, is the hamlet of Thorncombe Street with some nice cottages. Dr Fox died in 1962 two days after returning from Lake Como – 'I want to see it once more before I die,' he had said. Appropriately, the funeral service was in the church of St John the Baptist at Busbridge, in whose churchyard 30 years earlier was buried that great gardener Gertrude Jekyll. The church is a George Gilbert Scott junior design and also buried there are Miss Jekyll's brother and sister-in-law and her mother. Dr Fox's old home, Winkworth Farm, is now in the hands of the artist David Shepherd, best known for his elephant paintings and love of steam trains.

Busbridge Hall, a late 18th century house demolished in 1906 and replaced, is a wildfowl centre which draws many visitors. Crowds of a different kind travelled there in days gone by to watch leading cricketers, including overseas tourists, in action.

Lock cottage c. 1780, New Haw, nr. Byfleet

Byfleet

Brooklands, that famed home of early motor sport, is close to what is left of Byfleet's village identity. The track, with its steep banking, part of which has been reconstructed, was built in 1907 by Hugh Locke King, a motoring and aeronautics pioneer. In 1909 he opened an aerodrome in the middle of the $2\frac{3}{4}$ mile circuit. Vickers Armstrong took it over in 1936 and it was the site of important military innovations in World War Two, including the Wellington Bomber, one of which is now back at Brooklands to be part of a new museum of Brooklands' history.

C. Hawkins 1982

Byfleet Manor, Surrey.

34

A Bronze Age bucket and a hoard of Roman coins which were dug up in Byfleet are in the British Museum. The church of St Mary the Virgin is late 13th century, and one of its 18th century rectors was Stephen Duck who had earlier made the transition from Wiltshire labourer to Beefeater to the Queen and Keeper of a royal library at Richmond. He learned Latin and was ordained but in a fit of melancholy drowned himself in the Thames.

Royal Manor House was a royal hunting lodge but is now private apartments. Edward II stayed there frequently; the Black Prince lived there and stabled his horses at nearby Wisley; and legend has it that Henry VIII was nursed there as a baby. The house was rebuilt by Ann of Denmark but has since been reconstructed to such an extent that were she to return she would recognise only the gate pillars which have recently been listed.

Camberley ✣

Anthing that resembled a village disappeared a long time ago, but in days gone by when the military were becoming established there was a village atmosphere about the place. The Royal Military College was moved to Sandhurst, which is now a Berkshire village, in 1809 and York Town took shape. The name came from the Duke of York of nursery rhyme fame. The Staff College was built in 1862 and, it is said, Prince Albert caught his fatal chill watching its construction.

Capel ✣

Capel is a small village south of Dorking which was named after a capella or chapel that was used for worship in the 11th century.

The present church is largely 13th century and was originally dedicated to St Lawrence. Five hundred years later it was re-dedicated to St John the Baptist.

The parish once had a curate who wrote a charm against tooth-ache – and was probably thanked many times over in the days before the dentist's chair.

There is an old legend that if you walk around the churchyard yew here one hundred times at midnight a ghost will appear. What a pity that so few supernatural legends are as easy to verify!

The founder of the Quaker movement, George Fox, visited Capel in 1668 because of the district's involvement in the religion. It was brought to Capel by the Bax family in 1655 and Pleystowe, the house of Richard Bax, became home and local headquarters to the believers.

Caterham ✑

A town with some traces of the old village, and the administrative centre of Tandridge Council which came into being 16 years ago through a merger of the Caterham and Warlingham Urban District Council and Godstone Rural District Council. Caterham-on-the-Hill and Caterham Valley are the two components of the place, and the former will be remembered, not always with affection, by the guardsmen who have passed through the barracks. The depot was built in 1877 along with St Lawrence's Hospital and were forerunners of what is now a busy community. Caterham Valley grew up when the railway arrived in 1856 and the shepherds and quarrymen were gradually eased out. The old parish church of St Lawrence dates from Norman times and was disused from 1866, when St Mary's was built opposite, until 1927 when it was reopened.

Catteshall ✑

The riverside area to the east of Godalming has for centuries been dominated by the mill at Catteshall. It is thought to be one of three Godalming mills recorded in the Domesday Book – the others being Westbrook and Eashing – and has been thoroughly researched by local industrial archaeologists Alan and Glenys Crocker. The mill stands beside the road which winds through Catteshall, and beside the river which forms part of the Wey Navigation and runs through Godalming's historic open space known as the Lammas Lands. The research has been part of the work being undertaken on the restoration of the mill's water turbine which is said to be the largest and best preserved example of its type in the country, and one of Surrey's most significant industrial monuments. It is being restored by the Surrey Industrial History Group and Godalming Water Turbine Group.

Corn milling, malting, fulling, paper making, tanning, engineering, and foundry work have all been carried out at Catteshall. A significant date is 1838 when Thomas Sweetapple patented his invention of 'an improvement or improvements in the machinery for paper making'. Paper had been made in continuous rolls since 1803, and Sweetapple's improvements gave Catteshall a new lease of life through to this century when Albert Reed, whose name is synonymous with paper making, became the owner of what was then called Farncombe Paper Mills. Paper made at Catteshall was used by the *News of the World* and leading motoring and motorcycle journals. Reed continued to operate there until the 1930s depression when 100 local mill workers lost their jobs, and it was not until 1939 that engineers and founders took over the place.

There was Government work for 300 people during the war, but as peace returned the orders dwindled and only one-tenth of the wartime workforce was required by the 1970s. The mill was again sold and the present owners have helped with the preservation of equipment, including the turbine which had been installed in 1870.

Unsted Park is in the Catteshall locality, a late 18th century house which was built as Farley Hill. Memories of a downstairs maid at Unsted were published in the *Surrey Advertiser* early in 1984. 'The working quarters were the basement,' recalled the writer, 'and we never saw daylight. To me it was an immense place. They seemed to have endless servants. I never did see all of them. In my domain were capacious sinks and a large furnace which was lit by the odd job man, but I was warned if this went out I had to relight it, so I kept the blessed thing stoked up. The prospect of relighting it filled me with dismay so I made the water so hot it bubbled away and reached boiling point. When I started running it, it scalded my fingers which was the cause of my leaving.'

The period was just after the First World War, and the former maid continued: 'Besides loads of washing up and endless wide passages to keep clean with hearthstone, there were the copper saucepans to keep bright and clean, and that was a nightmare. After washing them I had to clean the insides with sand and the outsides with salt and vinegar to remove stains, and polish them afterwards. The only time I had off was every other Sunday afternoon when I finished all the washing up.' And she added: 'I worked from 5.30 am till late at night in dim light, and no fresh air, and it affected me.'

Chaldon

Close to the North Downs Way and the Greater London border, Chaldon attracts thousands of visitors because of a discovery made more than one hundred years ago. It was in 1870 that workmen renovating the 11th century church of St Peter uncovered a wall painting which sent experts and others into Victorian ecstasy.

The 12th century painting measures 17ft 2in by 11ft 2in and is 'archaeologically at least ... the most valuable and interesting wall painting in England'. It has as its theme the Ladder of Salvation. Its preservation was due to the rector at the time, the Rev. H. Shepherd, who kept an eye on the work and 'catching sight of some colour peeping out beneath the whitewash, warned those employed in removing the latter and thus preserved the painting from being destroyed', stated the Surrey Archaeological Society.

There is a plaque in the church with the following inscription:

Good Redar warne all men and women while they be here to be ever good to the poore and the nedy.
The cry of the poore is extreme and very sore
In thys worlde we rune oure rase.
God graunt us to be with Christ in tyme and space.

And there is a bell in the porch which is thought to have been cast as early as 1250.

Chaldon has a few old farms and a collection of more recent houses. It remains a fairly isolated community. It has had a history of water problems; the supply earlier this century was recorded as being small and intermittent and apt to fail in summer when the residents were dependent on shallow wells and ponds.

Charlwood 🦌

This border village has undergone as much change as any in the county because of the phenomenal growth of Gatwick Airport. London's second airport is at the village's back door, and the only thing that comes between the two of them is the county boundary. For while Gatwick has been transferred to Sussex, Charlwood successfully fought tooth and nail to remain in Surrey.

Before the big jets came to disturb the area, Charlwood was just a sleepy, peaceful village. Eric Parker, though, noted that it was being 'stiffened and discoloured' by building contractors as early as the first decade of this century, and while a village can to a point withstand the 'improvements' carried out by the building trade it surely cannot beat off the jet engine.

The Brighton road through the parish was part of the first road in Surrey to be made under the Turnpike Act in the reign of William III. But it was not until George II was on the throne that it was made into a 'driving road'. Gatwick racecouse was a well patronised place around the turn of the century after the track at Croydon had closed.

Agnes Dye's pregnancy probably saved her from the gallows in Elizabeth I's reign. The Charlwood spinster was found guilty in 1562 of the theft of 50s in money, a petticoat cloth valued at 13s 4d, and a sheet worth 5s. When she appeared before the judge he observed that she was with child and remanded her to jail where she remained until the following January when she was freed in a general pardon. Eleven years later another Agnes of Charlwood – it could even have been the same one – appeared in an Elizabethan sex scandal. Agnes Wood, a widow, was the mistress of one John Davie, a shoemaker, of Charlwood, who was charged with the rape of 10-year-old Anne Wood in Agnes' house, and was found not guilty at Croydon Assizes.

Chelsham 🌿

From St Leonard's church it was said you could see the Crystal Palace and the Greenwich Observatory. Chelsham is high up on the slopes of north-east Surrey and close to the boundary with Greater London. Buried in the churchyard is Thomas Kelly who looked after his father's sheep on Scotshall Farm when he was a boy, went to London at the age of 14 in 1786, became a publisher and eventually, in 1836, the Lord Mayor. The local boy who made good is remembered in the church by the Kelly Bible and Prayer Book. Kelly, who is buried under a yew tree, provided in his will for the distribution in Chelsham of a quartern loaf of bread on a particular Sunday, a benefaction to the priest who preaches on that day, and a gift for the school.

Chiddingfold 🌿

In the Middle Ages Chiddingfold was a great glass-making centre. There were eleven glass works on the village green in the reign of Elizabeth I, and the residents wanted them suppressed because they were a nuisance. Modern Chiddingfold knows nothing of glass-making, but some of its residents have been complaining lately about a 20th century industry: oil. When the well-diggers moved onto the rather oddly named Penang Farm some people had visions of a real-life Dallas on their doorstep. But the black gold was not found .

Chiddingfold is the largest of the Fold villages and draws thousands of visitors to its pretty centre where the green, pond, church, old houses and 14th century Crown inn come together. It is not difficult to imagine life back in the glass-making heyday. Chiddingford has a timeless quality to it even though traffic rushes through its heart. Glass from the village went into St Stephen's chapel at Westminster in 1351 and a few years later Edward III called for the best glass Chiddingfold could provide when he was building St George's Chapel at Windsor.

The Winterton Arms pub to the north of the village recalls the Earls of Winterton whose seat was at Shillinglee which is just over the county border in West Sussex. Shillinglee was the scene of great cricket matches in the middle of the last century (the ground is now part of a golf course) and Lord Winterton was an opening bat. In September 1847 he was batting against Farnham when a ball bowled by Frederick Caesar killed a swallow as it swooped across the pitch. His Lordship also played for Chiddingfold, two of whose players at that time became prominent enough to have their obituary notices published in Wisden. One was Alfred Hoar who left the village as a teenager to become a professional player. The other was James Sadler who was a member of a prominent Chiddingfold family. Wisden recorded in 1925: 'Like his father and grandfather he was a lover of the game. In his early days he had been invited to play for the county, but he preferred to restrict his activities to local matches in the west Surrey district. His death caused many interesting links with the past to be severed. He was, it is believed, the last survivor of the Shillinglee team which dismissed the Second Royal Surrey Militia without a run on August 13, 1855. For over 20 years he knew the great William Beldham well, and as a small child he had met Tom Walker, another member of the famous Hambledon XI, who died as long ago as 1831.'

James Charyngham was a Chiddingfold butcher who went to the gallows in Elizabeth I's reign because he stole a heifer valued at eight shillings. He was sentenced at Southwark sessions on November 7, 1560 after being found guilty of stealing the animal at night from a fellow villager, John Whyte.

Bonfire night is always a big occasion in Chiddingfold, with thousands celebrating in traditional style. Once, in 1929, the fire was set alight prematurely and the angry scenes which followed led to 250 police officers being sent to the village and a Justice of the Peace prepared to read the Riot Act.

Chilworth 🦢

Six men were killed in an explosion at the gunpowder works in Chilworth in February 1901. 'The most terrible accident which it has ever been our painful duty to record,' said the *Surrey Advertiser*. The explosion, soon after the men's breakfast break on a Tuesday, blasted the two-storey Black Corning House to pieces. It signalled the end of the village's long association with the manufacture of gunpowder.

There had been other explosions; one in 1763 brought down the tower of St Martha's church on top of the hill above the mill. Chilworth and gunpowder were together as early as 1580, but the Chilworth Gunpowder Company was not formed until 1885. Cobbett knew them and detested them. He thought the vale of Chilworth was 'exquisitely beautiful' and 'seems to have been created by a bountiful providence as one of the choicest retreats of man' but 'has been, by ungrateful man, so perverted as to make it instrumental in effecting two of the most damnable of purposes, namely the making of gunpowder and banknotes! Here, in this tranquil spot, where the nightingales are to be heard earlier and later in the year than in any other part of England; where the first bursting of the buds is seen in spring, where no rigours of season can ever be felt; where everything seems formed for precluding the very thought of wickedness; here has the devil fixed as one of the seats of his grand manufactory; and perverse and ungrateful man not only lends him his aid, but lends it cheerfully!'

Cobbett's broadside did not stop production. As many as 400 people were employed in the mills at their peak. The paper mill burnt down at the end of the 19th century. There was a mill listed in Domesday Book and corn and fulling mills were situated in Chilworth in 1589. In Charles I's reign the East India Company set up more extensive mills in the locality.

Chilworth today is a quiet village where history is unlikely to repeat itself. It has its fair share of visitors because of the hilltop church of St Martha, rebuilt by Henry Woodyer, the Surrey architect, in 1850. The earliest documentary evidence of the name is around 1200, and in 1463 Bishop Waynflete of Winchester wrote of 'the chapel dedicated to Saint Martha the Virgin and all the Holy

Martyrs, commonly called Martirhill founded and situated next to the town of Guldeforde in our diocese.' There is, according to the chaplain in a letter to the *Surrey Advertiser* in 1984, a strong tradition that early Christians were martyred there by pagan Saxons about 600 AD as part of the resistance movement to the spread of Christianity. If this were true, he wrote, then Martha could be a corruption of Martyr. 'Those of us connected with the church believe that the dedication of St Martha originated in Norman times and was a deliberate choice,' he added.

Chipstead ✄

The man who rose from labourer to builder of London Bridge is commemorated in Chipstead's 12th century church of St Margaret. Sir Edward Banks is said to have first observed the 'pleasant situation' of Chipstead when working on the railway at Merstham in 1803. Before he died in 1835 he had added the bridges across the Thames at Waterloo and Southwark to his impressive list of constructions.

Nearby is Kingswood which was once a well-wooded hamlet but is now built up and handy to the capital to make it popular with commuters. The church was built in 1852 and replaced one put up in 1835 soon after the village became a separate parish.

The church is dedicated to St Andrew while the one in Lower Kingswood, which was built in 1891, is to St Sophia. It was the work of two men who rejoiced in the names of Dr Edwin Freshfield and Sir Cosmo Bonsor and is, says Pevsner and Nairn, a 'most remarkable church, more even for its contents than its architecture'. There are nine Byzantine capitals which Dr Freshfield brought to Lower Kingswood. Three came from St John at Ephesus, and are either 4th or 6th century AD., and others come from Constantinople.

Brook Place, Chobham, built in 1656

Chobham

A 'grand military picnic' was held on Chobham Common in 1853 but it turned out to be the start of something more serious, for from that exercise came the decision to establish Aldershot as the Home of the British Army. Queen Victoria reviewed the troops at Chobham on June 21, 1853, and in 1901 a cross was put on the spot to mark the occasion and at the same time act as a memorial to the late monarch.

The camp was held from April until August and, said a writer of the period, was sufficient to prove the need for a more permanent school for field operations where officers might learn to handle large bodies of men, and where the men might learn to rough it, and to draw more upon their own ingenuity for comfort.

Chobham Common and Ridges have remained as military training grounds and are about five miles from the village where, in the early 19th century, there was a pig auction on Sunday mornings before church on land between the churchyard and the White Hart. St Lawrence's church dates back 800 years although it has been heavily restored. One of its monuments is to Sir Edward Banks who built Waterloo, Southwark and London Bridges. There is the tomb of Nicholas Heath, Archbishop of York from 1556-60, and Lord Chancellor of England under Queen Mary; he died in the Tower in 1578. He was described as a 'meek and modest' man and also an 'upright and brave man firm in his own convictions but tolerant of the religious opinions of others'. He refused to conform to the Elizabethan changes and resigned his See and went to live at Chobham Park which he had bought from Queen Mary for £3000.

At the time of the Domesday survey Chobham, or Cebeha, was held by Chertsey Abbey which had been founded as early as the seventh century. A church was recorded but no mills, although there is evidence of three such buildings on The Bourne brook.

Churt

Cobbett's plan to pass through Churt on a wild November night in 1822 came to nought when his guide became hopelessly lost. Today's travellers need have no fears for Churt is a modern village with a busy main road. However, get away from the A287 and there are many pleasant lanes and footpaths.

The hub of the village is the crossroads and the Crossways pub — one of the few inns in this south-west corner of the county which has altered little over the years. It was known at one stage as The Shant, supposedly on account of the landlady's repeated negative replies to proposals by her customers. One mile away is the Pride of the Valley inn, whose sign shows another pride of the valley, David Lloyd George, whose house, Bron-y-de, was close by. The fiery Welsh statesman was living in Churt in 1943 when he married his long-time secretary Frances Stevenson.

Lloyd George moved to Churt in 1921 and built Bron-y-de which is, alas, no more. His successful experiments in farming and fruit growing made him a popular figure in local agricultural circles, and he and his wife were in demand at shows and fetes.

Frensham Pond is fed by streams that come down through Churt. One flows from the slopes of Hindhead, past the Pride of the Valley and on to Silverbeck, near the junction of Jumps Road and the A287, on the corner of which was the old village post office. Another feeder stream flows from Hampshire into Surrey at Whitmoor Vale and continues on through Barford where there were at least three mills straddling the county boundary. Nowadays, it is a cut-off part of the village, known only to the few residents, ramblers and horseriders. Mr Hillier in his book, *Old Surrey Water-mills*, stated that a corn mill operated at Barford until the Great War, and that downstream there was a paper mill. But all of this has been lost in the mists of time, as has the area known as Upper Churt Common where, said Harry Baker in his *Frensham Then and Now*, ponies grazed in large numbers. The common began at Hatch Hill, where the road up from Churt ended at a gateway, and extended through what is now built-up Hindhead, across the Portsmouth road to Pitfold which was once the southern boundary of Frensham parish. There were herds of fallow deer, and it was the home of the black cock and grey hen, more commonly known as black grouse. According to Harry Baker the area of what is now the golf course at Hindhead — founded in the early part of the century and with Sir Arthur Conan Doyle as its president — was one of the favourite haunts of the black grouse. The birds were numerous on the heaths and moors of southern England but now they do not breed further south than Staffordshire. An interesting fact is that where conifers have been planted in vast quantities the black grouse has been making a comeback. Could they make a reappearance in Surrey as conifer replaces broadleaf in certain quarters?.

As we see more parcels of land being turned over to conifers it is easy to imagine a decline in deciduous woodland, but this is untrue says the Forestry Commission. In a paper entitled *Broadleaves in Britain* issued in 1984, it was stated that there had been no appreciable change in the area of broadleaved woodland over the last 30

Heron at Churt

years. Thirty-six per cent of Britain's wooded area is broadleaved; 58 per cent in England.

Churt's playing field is a First World War memorial, and before that the cricketers played near Frensham Pond when the captain often had difficulty getting all his players ready for the match. They lingered in the nearby hotel and it was not until a barrel of beer was taken to the ground that the skipper was sure of having eleven players present, but perhaps not always correct, at the appointed starting time.

Clandons

The twin villages of East and West Clandon are attractive and much-desired by home-seekers. West Clandon is nearer to the heart of Guildford, but the built-up area ends at Merrow and then comes Clandon Park. East Clandon is further along the A246 and has Hatchlands as its National Trust property.

Clandon Park is the home of the Onslow family who came from Shropshire in 1642 in the person of Sir Richard Onslow. Three members of the family have risen to the position of Speaker of the House of Commons. The house was built by the Venetian architect Giacomo Leoni in 1731, and the grounds were laid out by 'Capability' Brown.

West Clandon, which has been known as Clandon Regis and King's Clandon, has an attractive, winding main street along which is the low ceilinged Onslow Arms and the church of St Peter and St Paul. The latter is built on the site of a Domesday church and Aubrey observed that it had fallen down 'a small time before Xmas in 1716.' It was not completely destroyed and was rebuilt 'by the contributions of parishioners.'

Stories of the serpent at West Clandon are still told. *The Gentleman's Magazine* in 1796 carried the following account: 'A serpent once infested a back lane in the parish of West Clandon for a long time. The inhabitants were much disturbed and afraid to pass that way. A soldier who had been condemned for desertion promised, if his life was spared, he would destroy this serpent. Accordingly he took his dog with him. A fierce battle ensued, the dog fastened him and the soldier killed it with his bayonet in a field belonging to the glebe called Deadacre.' There is a carving at the church which purports to depict the engagement.

Between the two Clandons, wrote Eric Parker, 'the road runs by what is surely the finest ploughland in the county. A single field of over 100 acres stretches up the side of the down to a belt of firs.' Clandon Downs rise to the top of Newlands Corner and agriculture is still the predominant use.

East Clandon – once called Clandon Abbots – has the ancient church of St. Thomas of Canterbury which was a stopping-off place for pilgrims on their way to Kent. Hatchlands was built in 1758 for Admiral Edward Boscawen 'at the expense of the enemies of his country' according to a memorial to him in his native Cornwall.

Claygate 🌿

When the common at Claygate was enclosed in 1838 residential expansion soon followed, and when the railway came in 1885 the building boom really took off. Claygate is close to the Greater London boundary and therefore popular with commuters. The church of Holy Trinity was consecrated by the Bishop of Winchester in December 1840, local residents having built it when they found the nearest church at Thames Ditton too far away for regular worship. The new A3 sweeps around the east of Claygate, and travellers have a view of Ruxley Towers which was built in the 1830s as a country house and is now the headquarters of a trade union. During the Second World War Ruxley Towers was the headquarters of the NAAFI which was evacuated from London.

Cobham 🌿

Some would argue that Cobham is no longer a village, and they would probably be correct. In recent years there has been a housing boom and the old place is not the same. But Cobham of yesteryear is remembered fondly by the older members of the community. The broad sweep of the A3 by the White Lion public house and on up to Esher past the extensive grounds of the Fairmile Hotel are fading memories for motorists. Now, drivers rush past Cobham without hardly knowing it is there, carried on their way by a dual carriageway bypass.

The bridge over the Mole which once carried the main Portsmouth road was reputed to have been built for Queen Maud, who died in 1118. She was the wife of Henry I and the river crossing was said to be in memory of one of Maud's servants who drowned there. Rather improbable, as the contruction date is 1351, but in any case the bridge was rebuilt in 1782 to the design of the county surveyor of the time, George Gwilt. Two miles south-west of Cobham is the Hatchford mausoleum on Wisley Common, a domed temple erected by Sir Bernhard Samuelson in 1906. The copper top was stolen from the tomb in 1961.

Matthew Arnold, poet, critic, philosopher, lived in Cobham, at Painshill Cottage, from 1873-1888. Arnold was also a school inspector which befits the son of Dr Thomas Arnold, the legendary headmaster of Rugby School in Tom Brown's Schooldays. Painshill Park was created by Charles Hamilton, youngest son of the sixth Earl of Abercorn. Two presidents of the United States, Jefferson and Adams, were among the thousands of visitors who came out from London to wonder at Hamilton's work. Over the years the park became neglected but now, thanks to a preservation society, it is being returned to something like its former glory.

Cobham made the front page of the *Daily Mirror* in 1938 when a puritanical local councillor claimed that 'orgies' at local hops rivalled Sodom and Gomorrah. 'Dance morals trial held up by roars of village' screamed the *Mirror* in typical fashion. Girls and boys were 'cuddling and kissing in dark corners,' alleged the councillor. 'Rubbish' stormed the indignant locals at a hearing in the village. The elected representative was given a rough ride and eventually the young people of the village were vindicated. The hoo-haa soon died down.

Coldharbour

Leith Hill is the highest point in Surrey – at 967ft it tops Gibbet Hill at Hindhead by 72ft. And the tower on the summit rounds up the height to exactly 1000ft – a mountain in Surrey! The tower was built around 1765 by Richard Hull of Leith Hill Place. It comprised two rooms and a staircase, and when Mr Hull died in 1772 he was buried underneath and, if one story is to be believed, upside down so he might face his Maker the right way up.

The tower was vandalised and became the haunt of undesirable characters until, in 1796, it was filled with stones and cement. It remained that way until 1862 when it was restored, and is today, thanks to the National Trust, a popular place with visitors. Aubrey saw the 'whole county of Sussex, as far as the South Downes, and even beyond them to the sea; this entire county, part of Hampshire, Berkshire, and Nettlebed in Oxfordshire; some parts of Buckinghamshire, Hertfordshire, Middlesex, Kent and Essex; and by the help of a telescope, Wiltshire. It is much the highest eminence in this county (which has many other Alpes). The whole circumference cannot be less than 200 miles, far exceeding that of the keep and terrass at Windsor Castle, over which (as also the City of London, 25 miles distant) one sees as far as the eye, unarmed with art, is able to distinguish land from sky. The like, I think, is not to be found in any part of England, or perhaps Europe, beside.'

Ordnance surveyors in 1844 recorded 41 spires of London churches from the summit of Leith Hill which is close to Coldharbour, a small village at 750ft and therefore one of the highest in the county. The King's High Way, the old London to Arundel road, passed through Coldharbour, and on Gallows Hill criminals from the assizes at Dorking were hanged in the 17th century. Much earlier there was an Iron Age camp at Anstiebury which was again used during the Napoleonic wars to shelter women and children from Dorking while the men fought the French.

Compton

'Of the 25 parishes in England which bear the name of Compton, probably there is not one which can surpass Compton in Surrey in simple rural beauty, or in the interesting character of its church, an edifice which possesses the unique feature of a double sanctuary and also enshrines the oldest piece of Norman woodwork known in England.' That description appeared in volume XII of the Surrey Archaeological Collections following visits by members of the Surrey Archaeological Society in 1855 and 1861.

Compton's 'simple rural beauty' still exists in spite of the close proximity of the A3 trunk road and a busy main street. The church of St Nicholas is in a secluded corner, and has been described as the best of its style in England. It is approached from the east by a steep path which runs through a well tended churchyard whose level has been raised dramatically by burials in the 800 years before the village's present cemetery was consecrated in 1905. A plan to build a room to the north side of the church has split the community. Those opposed have argued that an addition would be harmful to the charm of the church and its surrounds, while those in favour con-

tend that the room would be seen by none but the hardiest explorer. The church council put forward the plan in 1982 but only in 1984 did the debate enter the public arena, and it rumbles on.

The village has become well known for its connections with the painter, G.F. Watts, who lived at Limnerslease in Down Lane. When he died at the turn of the century, his widow, Mary, had a memorial chapel and cloister built atop a hill overlooking the village. The striking red-brick chapel is built in the shape of a Greek cross and is reached by a winding, tree-lined climb. Beyond is the cloister where Watts is buried. The hillside has become the village burial ground and there can be few more impressively situated last resting places. Near to Limnerslease, which was built for Watts in 1891, is a Lutyens bridge which carried until recently the A3 Guildford bypass over the Pilgrims' Way. In the vicinity are tunnels in the chalk of the North Downs but the entrances have long been blocked up.

Just along the lane from the chapel is the Watts Gallery which houses many of the artist's works. That lane climbs to the eastern end of the Hog's Back and offers extensive views across Godalming, with the spires of Charterhouse School standing out above the trees, to Hindhead and Blackdown.

We will finish this piece as we began, with a quotation from the S.A.C. It is an extract from a petition to the House of Commons in 1640 that the vicar of Godalming be summoned to answer for his behaviour. One paragraph reads: 'That the said vicar and Mr Wayferar, Parson of Compton, in the said Countie of Surry, roade to Southampton, to eate Fishe and to make merrie together, and there (dyverse tymes) drank healthes to the Pope calling him that honest olde man.'

Cranleigh ✺

The locals proudly claim Cranleigh to be a village; some even say it is the largest in the country. In truth it is a town which retains some village charm. It was once a centre of the iron industry in Surrey and the Weald.

Cranleigh common, where cricket is played and a week-long family orientated tennis tournament is held every year, is close to the heart of the main street. Beside the common stands an hotel whose name is a reminder that Cranleigh was spelled Cranley until the post office, around the turn of the century, decided there was too much confusion for their staff with Crawley in Sussex.

Cranleigh was on the Guildford to Brighton line but following its closure the station was demolished and redeveloped. The railway ran through delightful countryside, much of which is now available to ramblers and riders, and passed through the station at Baynards before leaving the county. Baynards Park was built by Sir George More of Loseley in the late 16th century and destroyed by fire in recent years.

The first cottage hospital in England was opened at Cranleigh in 1859. Cranleigh Village Hospital was founded in October of that year by Albert C. Napper, MRCS, LSA, with assistance from the local rector, Archdeacon J.H. Sapte, who donated rent-free a small cottage which housed originally six beds and an operating room. Mr Napper practised in Cranleigh from 1854 to 1881 and had previously been in Guildford. Archdeacon Sapte was the incumbent at St Nicholas from 1846 to 1906. It is said that the cleric's gift was prompted by an emergency when Mr Napper had to amputate a man's leg in a nearby cottage after an accident in Cranleigh.

Cranleigh School was founded in 1864 and originally catered for 26 sons of farmers. It became a public school in 1898 and is now widely recognised. It stands outside the village on a road leading to Smithwood common where the Four Elms public house is set amid pleasant cottages.

Crowhurst

Queen Victoria and Prince Albert are reputed to have made a special visit from Windsor to view the wonder of this rural village: the yew tree in the churchyard. Surrey has so many gnarled old yew trees, each claiming to be famous, but the one at Crowhurst is arguably the king of them all. So it was most appropriate that the Queen of England should honour it with a visit.

The yew, which some say is 1500 years old, stands close to St George's church on a hill top north of the village. It is heavily shored and propped, but it probably looks better than it did a century ago when its trunk was a patchwork or iron and tin, the effort of villagers who thought they knew a thing or two about tree preservation.

The bole was hollowed out by a 19th century innkeeper and fitted with a circular table and seating for a dozen people. A door was fixed to the outside, and one exists to this day. On Palm Sundays in the old days there was always a fair around the much loved tree where 'ale flows free and mirth rises high.' Today, it and the churchyard have rather a forlorn appearance.

But it must have been much worse in the 17th century before 'part of ye body of Crohurst Church, which had lien in heaps a long time, was made plain and repaired.' The church, which probably dates from the 12th century, has memorials to the Gainsfords and the Angells, at one time the two big families in the district.

Dippenhall

This collection of houses and farms to the north-west of Farnham is just in Surrey, and was home to Harold Falkner the celebrated architect of Farnham. Falkner with the assistance of two labourers built nine houses at Dippenhall between 1921 and his death in 1963. One, Burles, comprises two barns brought from Gloucestershire and placed end to end. Falkner, contemporary of Lutyens and godson of Gertrude Jekyll, was a legend in his own lifetime, at least in Farnham. He was spoken of in hushed, reverential tones and to me, as a junior reporter on the *Farnham Herald*, he was a godlike figure. One hesitated to become involved in stories concerning Harold Falkner and it was, therefore, with some trepidation that I prepared for my first meeting with the great man. It must have been a year or so before the architect's death that my editor, the late Mr Theo Pope – a man whose feeling for the town of Farnham came through in every word he wrote – asked me to return some material to Mr Falkner, who lived in West Street and quite close to our offices. I was to knock and enter and proceed through to a back room where I would find Mr Falkner. It was a bright day but inside the architect's house it was dark and cheerless. A voice, weak with old age, called out. I traced it to the appropriate room, which was darker still, and as I announced myself I was unsure of the man's whereabouts. I needed to remain in that room no longer than it took to state my business and to this day I cannot say how he was positioned or indeed whether he was on a bed or a sofa.

Dittons

Long and Thames Ditton are beside the Thames and contain some rural charm. Indeed, Thames Ditton has been described as 'an oasis of old world survival'. It is the place where Eros, that statue in London's Piccadilly Circus, had its birth, in a foundry in Summer Road. In the churchyard of St Nicholas is the gravestone of Lady Pamela Fitzgerald, known as 'La Belle Pamela'. Her father, the Duke of Orleans, was guillotined during the French Revolution, and her husband, Lord Edward Fitzgerald, was shot by the English. Lady Pamela's half brother, Louis Phillipe, became King of France, and ended his days in exile at Claremont, Esher. She died in 1831 and was buried in Montmartre, but during the siege of Paris in 1870 a German shell wrecked her gravestone, and so her remains were brought to Thames Ditton. Another gravestone records the burial of Cuthbert Blakeden 'Serjeant of the Confectionary to King Henry VIII'.

Dockenfield

This hamlet is as far west as you can go in Surrey. The boundary with Hampshire meanders around it and often it is unclear just which county you are in. Dockenfield is hard by Alice Holt Forest which is over the border and was the home of Lord Baden-Powell, the founder of the Boy Scout movement, and much earlier the birthplace of this writer's ancestors. They were, in the main, farm labourers although the last one to live there, in the 1840s, was a tailor. For reasons yet to be discovered he took his family the six miles to Elstead and settled into a farming life there.

The Collyers were from Batts Corner which is between Dockenfield and Rowledge, and known to drinkers of real ale for the Blue Bell pub which was once a bakery – the ovens can still be seen. There is a nonconformist chapel at Batts Corner and the church of the Good Shepherd in Dockenfield whose war memorial is sheltered by a pitched roof. Dockenfield won a section of the county's best kept village competition a few years ago and it continues to have a clean look about it. The road to Frensham passes Frensham mill and climbs through Spreakley hollow where sand martins have long nested in the cliffs above the river.

Dormansland

A pleasant drive around the back of Lingfield racecourse brings you to Dormans railway station and then on to Dormansland. The station was opened in 1884 and was at first called Bellagio. Dormansland is a collection of cottages and houses along a main road but nearby are two important buildings. Greathed Manor was formerly Ford Manor and built in 1868 by Robert Kerr who wrote *The Gentleman's House*. Like so many of our larger old properties Greathed is now used for commercial purposes. Old Surrey Hall is right on the county border with Sussex and very close to the boundary with Kent. It was built around 1450 and underwent restoration in the 1920s. 'Imitation carried to the point of genius' said Pevsner and Nairn. 'The architect must have been working quite cut off from reality, and his flair for detail carries the onlooker over into the fairytale world.'

Dunsfold

As at Crowhurst, a much loved yew tree stands beside the church of St Mary and All Saints in Dunsfold. The churchyard is perfect peace, separated from the village by fields and woods. Peace, that is, when the jets are not flying low over the countryside from the nearby airfield. One of the pubs in the village was called, until recently, the Hawk and Harrier, which served as a constant reminder of the importance to British aviation that is attached to the aerodrome that takes its name from this sleepy village.

But back to the yew tree which is reputed to be 1000 years old. It certainly looks it, standing there by virtue of a multitude of props and wires. The setting of the church is completely rural, but so is the village. Dunsfold is off the beaten track and therefore largely unspoilt. Eric Parker wrote long ago of a Dunsfold lane ... 'a wild plum tree branching out of a hedge dressed with the whitest of delicate blossom, and in the white blossom, with the hot blue of a May sky beyond and between, a nightingale's throat throbbing with singing.' Those Dunsfold lanes still exist to delight the visitor; the nightingales may be harder to find.

In the reign of Elizabeth I the lanes would have resounded to the gossip of the locals when, in the fortnight before Christmas 1578, Thomas Mellersh was stabbed to death. His brother Harvey, a Dunsfold yeoman, was found guilty of the crime at Pond Close and sentenced to hang. Their sister Elizabeth and Elizabeth Burle, a servant of their father, were found guilty of being accessories. History does not record the motive.

Gertrude Jekyll, that great observer of the countryside in southwest Surrey, recorded a saying that was frequently heard in the district when praise was being accorded a man who was wide awake or more than ordinarily intelligent. 'He's got his head screwed on the right way,' ran the line which now has a more widespread use.

Eashing ✤

This sleepy hollow off the A3, through which the Wey meanders, was an important river crossing for centuries. The Romans knew it as they marched from the Weald to Wansdyke, a great fortification from Berkshire to the Bristol Channel. The bridge at Eashing, with seven arches, was built in the 13th century, almost without doubt by the monks from Waverley Abbey. The National Trust owns the bridge and the cottages near it, the latter bought for £400 in 1902.

A modern bridge takes the Godalming and Guildford bypass over the river a quarter of a mile above Eashing where, during construction of the road, skeletons were found. A Roman hairpin was lying near to the head of one of those buried who were thought to have died in times of peace.

There has been a mill at Eashing probably since the time of Domesday. Although Eashing was not named in the survey, Peper Harow was and it lies just across the main road. It seems likely that the mill at Pipereherge (and valued at 15s in 1086) was on the site of the present building, which is now an engineering works, at Eashing.

Downstream from Eashing the river turns towards Godalming and away from the neighbourhood of Hurtmore which has long been associated with market gardening. Hurtmore, too, was mentioned in Domesday as Hormera and had a mill valued at 11s. It has been suggested that the mill was one of Godalming's trio.

Effingham

Howard of Effingham School is a reminder of the connection the great sea-faring Howards had with this village between Guildford and Leatherhead. It was Lord Charles Howard, the second earl, who was most famous, for he was commander-in-chief of our fleet aboard Ark Royal against the Spanish Armada. His leadership brought victory and the title of the Earl of Nottingham in 1588.

Lord Charles's father, Lord William of Effingham, beat the Scots at Flodden Field. He was the son of the second Duke of Norfolk, and was granted Reigate Priory which had been built in the early 13th century for Augustinian canons. Effingham was sold by the third Earl of Howard in 1647.

Effingham today is a convenient place in which to live: handy shops, attractive houses, golf course, quick access to beautiful countryside, and, close by, a railway station on a loop line to London. The church is dedicated to St Lawrence and Aubrey noted in 1718 a small fair on the feast of the saint (August 10), but this event has long been abandoned.

A property in Lower Road is a Lutyens design and said to be one of the finest early houses from the Surrey architect. Recently in use as a convent, it was originally known as Red House and had a garden by that great Lutyens collaborator Gertrude Jekyll.

Egham

North of the bypass of this town is Runnymede, 182 acres of meadows which has given its name to the local council. Two important monuments draw tourists from all corners of the world. The Magna Carta was signed here in 1215 and is remembered by a memorial designed by Sir Edward Maufe and unveiled in 1957. It was in the Runnymede meadows that the all powerful King John, while staying at Windsor Castle, accepted the demands of his barons and signed the document that bestowed liberty and freedom on the country. On the slopes above is the Kennedy Memorial which was paid for by public subscription and unveiled by the Queen in 1965. The assassination of John F. Kennedy in Dallas in

1964 was one of those world events that will forever be remembered. The question, 'Where were you at the time?' will have been asked over and over again by visitors to Runnymede.

The Egham races were held in the riverside meadows during the 18th and 19th centuries. They were cancelled and not revived in 1886 when the police refused to provide officers to keep law and order at the track.

Elstead

It is likely the mill on the Wey was one of the six unnamed Farnham mills recorded in the Domesday Book, but no one can be sure. How many times has it been stated categorically that Elstead and its mill appeared in the survey of 1086? The mill is now a restaurant; just over 100 years ago it was a worsted factory employing 55 people. Since then, with its manufacturing life at an end, the mill house has had a variety of occupants, including the village policeman; a motoring pioneer, Mr Chaplin Court Treatt, who drove from the Cape to Cairo across the Sahara, and was given a tremendous homecoming with the village band at the head of the procession; and more recently one of the brothers Bentley of motor car fame.

The present mill is not the original building; that burnt down in the 17th century soon after Cromwell's troops had occupied it during the Civil War. Nearby, the bridge over the Wey has sections up to 700 years old but, sadly, its glory is partly hidden by the functional though ugly modern crossing which carries traffic into the village.

Elstead green has always been the focal point of the village, and around it stand some notable buildings, including Springfield Farm and the Woolpack. Between the green and the river is the Golden Fleece, another public house whose name recalls the days when Elstead's income came from wool.

The commons around the village have long been favoured for military training purposes, and during the wars were centres for billeting the troops. George V visited the soldiers during the First World War, leaving his car by St James's church and riding his horse down Westbrook Hill and on to Hankley Common. Lord Kitchener also reviewed the men but, in a *Farnham Herald* article in 1981, it was recalled that difficulties in lowering a flag were considered a bad omen. Soon afterwards Kitchener, the Secretary of State for War, lost his life at sea when on a visit to Russia.

Waverley Abbey's foundation charter in 1128 was the first time in which Elstead was named. Calling it Helestede, the abbey's founder, Bishop William Giffard, gave the Cistercian order near Farnham two acres of land. The church of St James was built about 1138 and served by the priests of Waverley. When the abbey was dissolved in 1536 Elstead, together with Seale and Frensham, became chapelries of Farnham. The first resident priest came to the village in 1829, but for much of the remainder of the 19th century the rector was a Yorkshireman, Joseph Rhodes Charlesworth, who, when he died in 1904, had completed 50 years as the parish priest. He was buried in the churchyard where a Cedar of Lebanon had been planted in 1849 as a thanks offering for relief from cholera which had spread death throughout the village.

There is a fine Lutyens house, Fulbrook, on the road to Cutt Mill, built in 1896 as a wedding present for Mr and Mrs Gerard Streatfeild. The builder was Andrew Chuter of Frensham who had built Pierrepont in his home village to the design of Norman Shaw. Mrs Streatfeild was the daughter of Mr Richard Combe of Pierrepont, and she worked with Gertrude Jekyll on the first garden. Her chauffeur was this writer's grandfather who had learned to drive in Hyde Park and, he always claimed, had been the first person to hold a driving licence in Surrey. Grandfather, who was 'volunteered' by his employers to drive a London bus in the capital during the General Strike, lived in the lodge at Fulbrook, which, say Pevsner and Nairn, is 'another stroke of genius on a tiny scale. One gable and a very tall bold chimneystack ... ' My father was born in the lodge and as a boy remembers that the cottage below the big house, Brookfield, was the laundry. It is now a private house and has been owned during the last 25 years by the late Peter Sellers, and Ringo Starr, the Beatles drummer. My days as a junior reporter on the *Farnham Herald* took me to Brookfield on the day Peter Sellers married the then little known actress Britt Ekland. The media jostled on the lawn as Sellers, in his best Goon voice, dominated a very public reception with a somewhat bemused Britt by his side. Sellers and Britt became popular figures in the village - often seen on bicycles - when he was recuperating from his first much publicised heart attack.

Englefield Green 🌿

This large village out towards Berkshire has on its outskirts the 'most ebullient Victorian building in the Home Counties', according to Pevsner and Nairn. Royal Holloway College on the A30 was built by W.H. Crossland in 1879-87 for Thomas Holloway. It was one of the first colleges for women (Girton was already open) and was the twin of Holloway Sanitorium at nearby Virginia Water. Crossland was a pupil of Sir George Gilbert Scott, who designed much in Surrey in the 19th century. Holloway made his fortune from the worldwide sale of Holloway's Pills. The college measures 550 feet by 376 feet and is built around a double courtyard in the French Renaissance style. It became a part of the University of London in 1900 and has admitted male students since 1965.

> 'Though deep, yet clear-though gentle yet not dull;
> Strong without rage; without o'erflowing full'

Those lines by Sir John Denham in 1643 were inspired by the view from Coopers Hill to the north of Englefield Green. The view is of Runnymede and the Thames and in addition to a large training college there is the Commonwealth Air Forces Memorial which was erected by the Commonwealth War Graves Commission. It commemorates the Commonwealth air force personnel who lost their lives in the Second World War. When the Queen unveiled the memorial in 1953 there were more than 25,000 relatives of the dead airmen present. On the slopes of Coopers Hill is the Kennedy Memorial and at the foot the Magna Carta Memorial.

Esher 🌿

The two big attractions which bring thousands of people to Esher are Claremont and Sandown Park racecourse. Lord Clive had Lancelot 'Capability' Brown and Henry Holland build the present Claremont in 1768, spending £100,000 on the house and gardens after pulling down the original property which had been erected by Sir John Vanbrugh in 1708 in the reign of Queen Anne. Vanbrugh called it 'Romantick' and sold it to the Earl of Clare (later the Duke of Newcastle). By a special Act of Parliament in 1816 it was purchased as a residence for Princess Charlotte on the occasion of her marriage to Prince Leopold. When she died Leopold continued to live there until he was elected King of the Belgians. Queen Victoria, who was Leopold's niece, spent much of her childhood at Claremont and the property eventually passed to her. The Monarch gave it to her youngest son, the Duke of Albany, and from there things became complicated because of the royal household's foot in both camps at the outbreak of the First World War. Eventually, Claremont was sold at auction and today it is one of Surrey's most visited estates.

Sandown Park racecourse has also had its share of royal patronage since it was established in 1875 on the site of one of Esher's three historic manors which was called Sandon. A 12th century church hospital had been situated there and this had merged with St Thomas's in London in the 15th century before being confiscated by the Crown.

Ewhurst 🌿

A Roman villa at Rapsley to the north of this village was discovered in 1956. Its date of occupancy has been put at 80-350 AD and the inhabitants probably made tiles and raised stock. The villa was unearthed when Hareholt Copse was being replanted, and archaeologists completed the work in 1968. Evidence of a Roman road through the parish has been proved as an offshoot of Stone or Stane Street.

The mill at Ewhurst was, at 800 feet above sea level, a notable landmark, but it ceased work in 1885 and was converted into a house around the turn of the century.

'Tinkering repairs' to the ancient central part of the tower and its wooden steeple in 1839 brought the lot crashing down, and the church of St Peter and St Paul was mostly rebuilt.

North-west of the village is the Hurtwood, high, wooded ground with some fine houses, one of which, Long Copse, was considered by G.F. Watts, the Victorian painter who lived at Compton, to be the most beautiful in Surrey.

Farleigh

On the map the boundary with Greater London forms an umbrella above Farleigh up in the north-east corner of the county. It is drawn in that fashion thanks to the fighting qualities of the local residents, for Farleigh was intended to be included in the London Borough of Croydon when the local government boundaries were changed in the 1970s.

In 1908 Farley, as it was spelt, caught Eric Parker's attention. He wrote of the tiny church by a fine farmyard where all was not well, in his opinion. 'Its modest spire, as you walk to the churchyard, is dominated and affronted by the hideous clock tower of a neighbouring lunatic asylum. Why should such a thing be?' he asked. 'County councils have decreed that in this part of Surrey must be massed together the thousands of poor souls who have lost the reason which county councillors must be supposed to possess; but why insist on their unhappy presence? A building to hold such sadness should be a quiet thing, hidden among trees, silent, alone. But that would suit neither councillors nor architects. For them, asylums must stare, scar, insist that they will be seen and known; and here, in what should be tranquil and lovely country, they violate the hills!' The words of Eric Parker in 1908.

Farley Green 🐚

Those two great writers on Surrey, Aubrey and Bray, brought this area to the notice of a wider audience in 1672 and 1803 respectively, but it was not until Martin Tupper discovered the 'Roman Temple' on Farley Heath that one of the south's finest Romano-British camps was determined. Farley Heath was known as 'Little Surrey Pompeii' when Tupper, between 1839 and 1847, spent 'random hours grubbing' with encouraging but inconclusive results.

Then between February and July 1848, he supervised three men from the nearby estate of the Duke of Northumberland who worked continuously and made many interesting discoveries. An Albury schoolmaster, Mr Lovell, 'grubbed' in December 1852 and found British coins and a horse's bit, and much later, in 1926, Mr S.E. Winbolt, dug there and found pottery.

The importance of the camp at Farley Heath, which had been known as Old Bury, hence the name Albury, kept the archaeologists busy and further digging in 1939 was interrupted by the start of the war. Many of the discoveries are on display in Guildford Museum.

Non-conformist worship in Farley Green is almost 100 years old, and its origins are simple. The story goes that a Gomshall man, Mr Abel Overington, and his two sons walked the three miles to Farley Green one Sunday afternoon in 1888 to attempt to interest the people in a spot of preaching and hymn singing. When the visitors arrived they found everyone out on the green, but it was not a welcoming party. The men and boys were playing cricket, while the womenfolk were watching. Typical of many a village green in high summer.

Mr Overington was undaunted. He told the people of his intent and several joined him for an open-air service in one corner of the green. One of his boys led the singing on his flute, and a resident brought chairs from her cottage. The gathering was such a success that Mr Overington returned the following week and for the next two summers. Then a cottage was offered for winter services, and eventually, with the pioneering Mr Overington moving on, the congregation came more under the wing of the chapel in Gomshall.

Farncombe 🦢

There is definitely a village 'feel' about this appendage of Godalming which was recorded in the Domesday Book as being held by the Bishop of Bayeux. It is separated from its bigger neighbour by the Lammas Lands, riverside meadows where for centuries cattle have grazed.

Farncombe was the birthplace of one of the heroes of the *Titanic*, the ill-fated liner which struck an iceberg and sank on its maiden Atlantic voyage in April 1912. Jack George Phillips was the chief wireless operator on the ship and by remaining at his post sacrificed his life. In Godalming, the Phillips Memorial Garden, designed by Thackeray Turner and laid out by Gertrude Jekyll, is an everlasting reminder of this brave man. There is also a memorial to him in Farncombe's St John the Evangelist church where he was a choir-boy.

The church was built in 1847 and, according to the *Surrey Advertiser* in 1922, stands on what was known as the 'Field of Blood' because it was the site of the execution in 1840 of a youth who had poisoned his uncle.

Red-bricked almshouses alongside the main road were built in 1622 by Richard Wyatt, a wealthy benefactor who lived at Hall Place, Shackleford. Wyatt was Master of the Carpenters' Company in the City and laid down that an 'Oyspitall' be built for 'tenn poore men.'

Opposite the almshouses are extensive playing fields where once stood Broadwater House, home of the Marshalls, and renowned for its cricketing links. There was a fine ground at the house on which many of the great 19th and early 20th century players performed. The Marshall brothers, the Hon. Alexander and the Hon. Frederick, were prominent members of the local cricket scene in the middle and second half of the last century, and their hospitality was well-known. In 1852 an England XI played there and the great player of an earlier age, William 'Silver Billy' Beldham, then aged 86, walked the seven miles from his home at Tilford to watch the game. He was, in that year, described as possessing 'a perfectly upright bearing, looked to be about 70 years old, used a stick in walking, and had a profusion of white silvery hair of considerable length, dropping down to his shoulders. His complexion was remarkably fresh and ruddy and, notwithstanding his great age, he was even then a splendid specimen of a veteran athlete.'

Broadwater Lake is a popular spot with anglers who ring its banks and frequently catch some of the big specimens that lurk in its depths.

Felbridge

The Evelyn family have roots in this village down on the Sussex border just north of East Grinstead. They lived at Felbridge Place and would have been involved in the formation of a separate ecclesiastical parish at the time St John the Divine church was built in 1865. The Weald iron industry was strong in this area and mill ponds are a reminder of that age. North of Felbridge is Newchapel where the first European church of the Latter-Day Saints (the Mormons) was built in 1958. Newchapel House was put up in 1908 for the Pears Soap boss.

Fetcham

A book published 50 years ago said of Fetcham that it was 'rapidly filling up'. Well, in the subsequent half a century it has achieved its quota and some would say spilled over. Fetcham can hardly be classed as a village now; more a suburb of Leatherhead and a continuation of Great Bookham. In days gone by though it was divorced from its neighbour and as rural as the next village. The river Mole has played a large part in the life of the community and its presence still forms an effective boundary between Fetcham and Leatherhead.

At the time of Domesday Fetcham boasted five mills, had a one-sixth share in another and a one-third stake in a seventh. Part of St Mary's church may be pre-Conquest, and a Saxon cemetery was discovered during building work in the neighbourhood. Another old building is the Old Rising Sun restaurant which has a 1348 date linked to it but is more likely to be 15th century. For years it was an ale house and beer was brewed on the premises using local hops. That was an industry to be found throughout Surrey, for in addition to the acres of hop fields there were small areas of bines which were grown to produce local beers. The custom has returned in the last decade with the upsurge in interest and support for real ale.

Among those buried in the churchyard are Admiral Sir George Henry Richardson, who was well known as a hydrographer and expert in submarine telegraphy, and Sir Francis Graham Moon, who was a printer and publisher and Lord Mayor of London in 1854. His eldest son, Sir Edward Graham Moon, was rector of Fetcham from 1859 until his death in 1904.

The mill pond at Fetcham caught Eric Parker's imagination. It was 'unlike any other pond I know. It is two or three hundred yards long and perhaps eighty yards wide, slopes gradually from the sides over a chalky bottom, and is of an intense clear green.' He was fascinated by the 'uncanny motion' of the water. The springs have since been harnessed by a water company and are now under manholes but visible to anyone who cares to ask the right question.

Forest Green

Open-air services with the preacher using a farm wagon as a pulpit were a common sight around these parts a century or so ago. The Sunday afternoon missionaries used to thump out the message as the tide of non-conformism swept over the southern part of the county. In June 1878, though, steps were taken to build a chapel, and Master John Evelyn, son of the lord of the manor, was led along by his nurse to lay a memorial stone. Soon the building was ready for use and the faithful had a permanent home for their services.

There was a track from Forest Green over the back of Leith Hill which was known as Smuggler's Way, and contraband aplenty was shipped towards the capital through the thickly wooded countryside. The Oke stream springs up at Pitland Street on the eastern slope of Holmbury Hill and at High Ashes on the western slope of Leith Hill and flows past Forest Green and nearby Oakwood Hill to meet other tributaries and form the north branch of the Arun in Sussex.

Frensham ❧

Everyone's heard of Frensham Pond. At least it seems like it on a summer's day when the sand beside this large expanse of water resembles Brighton on a bank holiday. Few of the visitors, though, will know of the pond's and the district's history.

Frensham Great Pond, to give it its correct name, and to distinguish it from its smaller neighbour, was noted as early as 1208 when it belonged to the Bishop of Winchester and provided him with fish for his table in Farnham Castle. Almost two miles in circumference, it covers the site of a natural pool which was subsequently enlarged. Bowen's map of 1749 recorded that Frensham had 'springs not inferior to those of Tunbridge Wells.'

The first seaplane was tested on the pond in 1913 and while that was a happy and successful occasion there have been many sad times when bathers have drowned. Local children have the dangers of the pond spelled out: its varying depth close into the shore and its hidden weed. But visitors do not know of these hazards and all too often tragedy has ended a day out in the country.

Across the main road and over King's Ridge lies the Little Pond which was formed in 1246. It, too, provided fish for the bishops, while a third and now almost unknown mere called Abbot's Pond at nearby Tilford was created to supply the monks of Waverley Abbey. The dam of that pond burst in 1841 and was never restored; the stream being dammed lower down to create the present Stockbridge Pond.

During the Second World War both ponds at Frensham were drained to prevent them from being a directional aid to enemy bombers as they lined up for raids on military targets at Aldershot and Bordon. Local residents can recall retrieving the fish as the water drained away.

Frensham Great Pond
from The King's Ridge.

The parish of Frensham is far-flung but small when compared with former days when it not only included Churt but Hindhead and Shottermill as well. Millbridge crossroads have never aligned and for years there was a white stone on the roadside which caught out many a motorist. It was originally placed there when the Farnham to Hindhead road was made and intended to keep heavy wagons and their loads from bumping into the house on the corner.

Pierrepont is now a school but until the last war it was a private house, being owned by the Combe family who were members of the Watney brewing concern. The last lady of the house was a Lady in her own right and went to extraordinary lengths to let people know. She was The Lady Constance Combe and many a soul committed the unforgivable sin of omitting the definite article. Tradesmen were even sent back from whence they had come if the parcel they bore did not include that three letter word.

St Mary's church is old but little remains of the church first built on the site in 1239. It is situated above the river and close to some lovely old cottages. A large cauldron in the church has confounded people for centuries. Did it belong to Mother Ludlam, the Waverley witch? Or was it once in the kitchen of Waverley Abbey? We will probably never know.

Friday Street ✏

'You turn a corner of the road and you are in Switzerland', said Eric Parker, rather extravagantly, of Friday Street. It is indeed a beautiful place with a pond, some cottages and an inn. In pre-motor car days it was probably more romantic with the smell of wood smoke filling the valley. If the Wotton mill was here the pond may well be the result. The 11th century miller ground corn; later iron, wire and gunpowder were made in this quiet spot. The powder mill was established during the reign of Henry VIII and was said to be the first of its kind in England. Rocque's map of 1762 recorded a mill pond but not a mill.

The inn is named after Stephen Langton, the Archbishop of Canterbury in King John's time whose image is depicted in a set of three inch high carved heads above the south door of Wotton church.

Frimley Green ✏

The bustling area that includes Mytchett, Deepcut and Frimley is a far cry from the days when there was more heather than houses. The heaths are still there but at arm's length. This is now firmly commuter land. There are no highwaymen on the barren heaths and no caves in the sand where the booty was hidden. It was a place with a gibbet but the last public execution was in 1850 when three men hanged for the murder of the parish priest in the Parsonage – which was said to be haunted for years after.

The railway and the canal opened up the district, but the two did not always go together. Once, the aquaduct carrying the canal over

the railway sprung a leak and had to be closed because the escaping water was damping the fires in the engines passing underneath. The Basingstoke Canal was cut through Frimley Green upon the conclusion of the War of Independence, although the work had been authorised by an Act of Parliament in 1778. Ten years later a private company using Irish labour began the work and the canal was opened in 1796. It is 37½ miles long, has a width of 26ft, and was 4½ft deep. The 15-mile stretch from the Wey to the Hampshire border rose 195ft through 28 locks. Road and rail transport put paid to the canal as a profitable means of shifting cargo, and it fell into disrepair, but fortunately, for the good of the environment and the community, the waterway is being restored.

Ethel Smyth, a celebrated composer and pianist, who died in 1944, went to Frimley school after moving to the village in 1867, at the age of nine, when her father took a command at nearby Aldershot.

Gatton

You will not find a village here but it is a place with a good deal of history attached to it. It once returned two members to Parliament and earned the wrath of Cobbett who called it a 'very rascally spot of earth.' It was a Rotten Borough but the Reform Act of 1832 put a stop to all that, and upset the plans of the new owner, Lord Monson, who, only two years earlier, had paid £100,000 for the estate and the power that went with it.

The Domesday Book recorded a church at Gatton, but the present one, dedicated to St Andrew, is 13th century. Lord Monson, who was the fifth baron, filled it with treasures from Europe during the 1830s. In the park is what has been called the smallest town hall in Britain, built in the form of a portico in 1765 and from which Gatton's owner sent the two MPs to Westminster.

Monson's mansion was burnt down in the 1930s but not before Sir Jeremiah Colman, of mustard fame, had been an owner. Today, Gatton is popular with walkers following the North Downs Way, and the old park has been bisected by the M25.

Godstone

Cobbett took this village to his heart but he would surely shudder today. He found peace and quiet in the White Hart which is still a comfortable inn overlooking the green but too close to a busy road junction for comfort. Godstone is on the A25 and has a raceway of a one-way traffic system around its centre where the A22 comes in from the south.

'Godstone,' wrote Cobbett in 1822 'is a beautiful village, chiefly of one street with a fine large green before it and with a pond in the green. A little way to the right (going from London) lies the vile Rotten Borough of Bletchingley, but, happily for Godstone, out of sight. At and near Godstone the gardens are all very neat and, at the inn, there is a nice garden well stocked with beautiful flowers in the season. I saw here, last summer, some double violets as large as small pinks, and the lady of the house was kind enough to give me some roots.'

The march of time has changed Godstone. But the gardens are still pretty and the green and the pond are still opposite the inn. The White Hart was probably built in the reign of Edward II and altered in the Elizabethan period. At one time it was known as the Clayton Arms after Sir Robert Clayton, the son of a carpenter from Northamptonshire. Clayton made his money as a scrivener and became Lord Mayor of London. By the time he died in 1707 he was the biggest landowner in the district of Godstone and Bletchingley in whose church there is a memorial.

A prize fight at nearby Blindley Heath in 1815 is thought to have brought the Czar of Russia and his entourage to stay at the White Hart.

Godstone in very recent times has been pinpointed as one of several locations in the county where good quantities of oil are thought to be beneath the surface. Four hundred years ago it was the centre of the Surrey leather trade. Godstone, it seems, has always been a busy centre, and one which needed to rebuild after being devastated by the Black Death.

The appropriately named Walker Miles, who was a pioneer of rambling clubs, is buried at Godstone in the churchyard of St Nicholas, which was restored in 1872 by Sir George Gilbert Scott who lived at Rooksnest nearby. He also was responsible for St Mary's almshouses to the south of the church.

Two yeoman from the village were hanged in Elizabethan times for attacking one Michael Knight in the highway. Lewis Hobbye and Matthew Bone were the defendants and Hobbye was said to have thrust at Knight with a staff and inflicted injuries from which he died the following day. A jury found them guilty on November 10, 1582.

Gomshall 🦋

Tanneries, which closed in 1988, have dominated this small village on the A25. Rebuilt and expanded after a fire in 1890, they were known to visitors from around the world. Two main road pubs are the Black Horse and the Compasses. The Black Horse was probably a malthouse at the end of the 17th century and was a brewery into this century. The Compasses was built in 1830 and was originally a beer shop, transferring to an inn about 100 years ago. King John House on the corner of Queen Street and the main road was, according to local legend, built shortly after the plague in 1666 on the profits of hides collected in London.

The village was Gomeselle in the Domesday Book when there was a mill, but not the mill building of today.

Gomshall was in the Blackheath Hundred and in 1086 there was land for 20 ploughs, 30 villagers and eight smallholders with 18 ploughs, and six slaves. The mill was valued at 40d, there were three acres of meadow and woodland with 30 pigs. The survey pointed out that 'the villagers of this village are exempt from all the Sheriff's concerns'. It added that the Bishop of Bayeux wrongfully placed half a hide of land of the manor in the manor of Bramley, and held it. It was in Gomshall before and after 1066. And in neighbouring Wotton Hundred the King had a hide in lordship which 'lies in the lands of Gomshall'.

Grayswood

The people of Grayswood gathered almost as one against the coming of the oil men earlier in the decade. Seismic tests concluded that substantial deposits of gas were contained deep in the sub-strata, and there was talk of Holmen's Grove becoming the biggest on-shore gas field in the country. It all came to nought, though, after exploratory drilling, but the locals now have a deeper respect for their environment. The site pinpointed was in a valley north of Grayswood on the A286 where All Saints church looks out on to the cricket green and Prestwick Lane which runs away to Chidding-fold is thought to be a modern corruption of Priest's Way.

Grayswood was part of Witley ecclesiastical parish up to the turn of the century when, through the generosity of a local man, Mr. Alfred Hugh Harman, a church and vicarage were built. An architect from nearby Haslemere, Mr Axel Haig, drew up the plans and work began in February 1901. A year later the church was consecrated. Mr Harman. who lived at Grayswood Place, is remembered by a memorial tablet in the church, while both he and his wife are buried in the churchyard where there is an impressive memorial stone.

Local men who lost their lives in the wars are recalled on a memorial beside the road to Haslemere and which looks over a valley towards Hindhead. It is a beautiful spot and I am forever reminded of an old countryman's saying about it, when talking about thunderstorms. He said, in his rustic accent: 'When thaat thunder gets stuck in thaat vaalley it don't come out too easy.' The road to Haslemere climbs steadily from the Wheatsheaf public house; it is thought to have been made in 1757 and not so long ago was quite a test for motor vehicles.

Hale

Heavy traffic rumbles through this hillside village to the north of Farnham and takes away much of the natural charm. This state of affairs has been the topic of conversation for generations. Hale people have always been a tough breed and weathered every storm, but the 18th and 19th century buildings are suffering under the strain, and there is rightly concern being expressed. One building still going strong is the Bethel Chapel in Bethel Lane which celebrated its 150th anniversary in 1984. It was built in 1834 on a site where preachers had long attracted crowds to their open air services, and the opening ceremony hymn was specially written by the man who was to become the first headmaster of Hale school.

A public house that overlooked the recreation ground was taken over during the Second World War and never again was a pint served there. It was known as the Sir Colin Campbell and was home for the Hale Brass Band. Then, with the outbreak of war, it became a rescue depot and the men on duty slept on bunks in the former cellar, and often shared their vigil with Canadian soldiers who were stationed in the area. Hale has always played a major part in the story of brewing in the Farnham district, and when The British Grenadier disappeared in 1900 it was probably one of a score of houses which lost their licences in a magisterial crackdown, brought about, it was suggested, when one member of the bench joined the temperance movement.

Modern Hale is dominated by a massive housing development at the top of the hill, but the heart is still around the recreation ground which borders the main road. There, the competitive Hale sportsmen have been tough opponents over the years at both football and cricket. 'The men from the hill' as they were dubbed at the turn of the century.

One of their best cricketers then was the vicar, the Rev George Edward Hitchcock, who devoted himself to the life of the parish for 16 years from 1894. Another fine batsman from these parts was Albert Baker who was good enough to play alongside the legendary Jack Hobbs in Surrey's opening partnership in the county championship for several seasons in the early part of the century.

When the Great War broke out in August 1914 it was to the door of Hale Institute that a notice was pinned and read: 'It is supposed the Farnham Ramblers were engaged with the Germans, which is more important than cricket.' The Ramblers were a team of businessmen who played in Farnham Park and sometimes at Hale, whose ground is just outside the boundary of the park, a wide expanse on the slopes above Farnham. Once the property of the Bishops of Winchester who lived in Farnham Castle, it is now controlled by the local council. A popular walk from Hale crosses the park to emerge at the stile and alley described by George Sturt in his autobiographical *A Small Boy in the Sixties*.

Hambledon

A law of the land had its origins in Hambledon back in 1933 when the members of the Women's Institute branch won the approval of their colleagues from all over the country on the question of the sale of live English wild birds. Hambledon's resolution was passed unanimously by 8000 women attending the Institute's national conference in the Albert Hall, and later that year a Bill was adopted by the Prime Minister, Mr Ramsey Macdonald, as a Government measure, and became law. But the original credit went to the women of

Hambledon for bringing the matter to the notice of the public at large. The motion was proposed by the daughter of the author, Eric Parker, who lived in the village, but sadly his wife, who was president of the WI branch, died on that very day having collapsed the previous day while travelling to London by train to hear her daughter speak in the Albert Hall.

A clay track through Hambledon Hurst was the old highway between Godalming and Chiddingfold and was continually presented as being out of repair in Godalming Hundred courts in the 14th, 15th and 16th centuries. On September 21, 1340, Thomas le Beel, rector of Hambledon, came before the court for digging a ditch in the highway.

Nowadays, Hambledon is known for its brick-making; centuries ago iron was mined, hence the name Mine Pits Copse. The ore was mined by Lord Montague who ran into a spot of bother in February 1570 when commoners resented his cutting the woods for his works.

In the 1930s there was great concern when the Godalming fire brigade refused to attend a rick fire in the village. The reason? The owner of the rick was not a subscriber to the brigade. There was alarm in the village when it was discovered the parish council had also not been supporting the brigade, which would be within its rights not to attend a house fire. The outcome? It was suggested that Hambledon enter into an agreement with Guildford 'as the contribution was lower than that required by Godalming, and the extra four miles made very little difference with a motor fire engine', reported the *Haslemere Herald*.

St Peter's church sits atop a knoll at the end of a lane and within its ground are two venerable yews, one of them hollow and the subject of a piece of Surrey folk lore. It was said that if you walked three times around the inside of the hollow tree you would see a witch.

Hambledon is an out-of-the-way place which until the mid-1970s, lent its name to the local authority. Hambledon Rural District Council was one of the bodies which was swallowed up when the Local Government Commission reorganised the boundaries. Waverley District Council was the new baby, and in 1984 a royal charter gave it borough status and thus a mayor.

Hascombe ✤

Hascombe seems to be cut off from the outside world. It is a beautiful village surrounded by heavily wooded hillsides. And recently, for good measure, it has acquired a vineyard producing a vintage which proudly carries the village's name. The trees have been noted by a succession of writers. One in the 19th century said of the chestnuts at Burgate: 'Such a bit of Spain as it would be difficult to parallel this side of the Pyrenees.' Those chestnuts are now on private property, but there are others, especially along the winding lanes of the village towards Hydon Ball, a curiously named beauty spot which, from its 593ft summit, offers superb views over the Weald.

Eric Parker thought the yews in the churchyard would one day be famous but, alas, he was wrong. They are no longer there, apart from a small archway at the gate. St Peter's church was rebuilt in the mid-1800s and is tucked away behind the village street in a peaceful setting. Opposite is the village pond and an old cottage which was once an almshouse. Nearby, the White Horse formerly had a sign which had been painted by Gertrude Jekyll who trained as an artist but was more renowned in these parts as a gardener whose work was to be seen complementing the many Lutyens designed houses.

Hascombe Hill is 51ft higher than Hydon Ball and was important as a telegraph station at the dawn of the 19th century (much earlier it was an Iron Age fortress). For 20 years the shutter system of sending messages between the Admiralty and Portsmouth involved a great deal of manpower, and the Hascombe telegraphists were a vital link in the chain.

Four hundred years ago Thomas Hedger went to the gallows for sheep stealing. He was a Hascombe butcher and was found guilty, with a Cranleigh man, William Kerrey, of stealing 69 sheep. Hedger was sentenced to hang on June 30, 1579, at Kingston Assizes. Kerrey was also found guilty but was handed over to the clergy. Later he was indicted on similar offences but, according to the record, was 'at large' at the time of his scheduled appearance in the dock.

Haxted ✎

A hamlet in the parish of Lingfield within a mile of the Kent border, and visited by large numbers because of its watermill museum. Haxted mill dates from 1680 but there was a mill in the 14th century according to the will of Reginald de Cobham of Starborough Castle. The present mill ended its working life in 1945 and opened as a museum in the late 1960s. The river Eden powers the wheel which is about 150 years old.

Headley ✎

The M25 motorway cuts through the countryside between Headley and its neighbour Walton-on-the-Hill. The section of London's southern bypass between Reigate and Wisley took a long time to be completed and was opened in 1985.

Headley, high up on the chalk, attracted Aubrey on one of his perambulations, and he wrote: 'The shepherds of these Downs use a half-horn, slit length way, nailed to the end of a long staff with which they can hurl a stone to a great distance and so keep their sheep within their bounds, or from straggling into the corn.' And William Bray, who completed the massive county history begun by the Rev. Owen Manning, spoke to a man in 1808 who remembered, 40 years earlier, shepherds in the area who could hit sheep at a distance of 20 rods.

The church of St Mary the Virgin is Victorian but evidence of an earlier building can be seen over the grave of one of the 19th century incumbents, the Rev. Ferdinand Faithfull, who died in 1871. Faithfull's daughter, Emily, who was born in 1835, became printer and publisher to Queen Victoria after she had gone to London and set up a printing press.

Walton-on-the-Hill was in the spotlight in 1981 when the Ryder Cup golf tournament was held at Walton Heath. Few of the thousands of visitors to that event would have given a second thought to St Peter's church in which there is an 800-year-old lead font, the only one in Surrey and one of only 30 in England. Thirteenth century Walton Place, which lays claim to being the oldest house in the county, was once home to Anne of Cleves.

Heath End 🌿

The Halfway House pub on the main road at Heath End probably owes its name to the First World War, perhaps much earlier. It has been suggested that it was halfway between the railway station at Farnham and the military centre at North Camp, Farnborough, and troops on the march to or from the trains welcomed its appearance through the dust and dirt of a weary trek. A photograph in the *Farnham Herald* recently showed the Halfway House in 1905, a building whose doors opened directly on to a dusty road. Opposite was a bakery and a tearoom. Now the road is choked by fast-moving traffic and local residents are rightly concerned about the associated dangers, and their campaign for an improvement is linked with the need to find a better road system around Farnham.

Hersham 🌿

A pleasant enough suburb of Walton-on-Thames but it rarely gets a mention. The common was enclosed in 1804 by an Act of Parliament and this was the signal for the developers to take an interest. Wealthy Londoners had villas built at Hersham in the 1820s, the railway arrived in 1838 and soon a busy and thriving community was established. A nonconformist chapel went up in 1844 but St Peter's church was not built for another 43 years. The chapel has been demolished as has its neighbour, Rookwood, a circular cottage built with the trunks of gnarled trees.

Hinchley Wood 🦋

Suburban Surrey beside the Kingston bypass. In fact, the area was settled when the new road opened it up in the late 1920s, and when the railway station was opened the name Hinchley Wood (already in use for a local group of trees) became accepted. Telegraph Hill was known as Cooper's Hill in the days when there was a semaphore station there in the early 1800s.

Hindhead 🦋

People know Hindhead for a variety of reasons but not, perhaps, for the one that led to the existence of the hilltop village. The name of Professor John Tyndall does not ring too many bells nowadays, but this eminent scientist of the 19th century was the person who can fairly be said to be the founder of modern Hindhead.

It was Tyndall, one hundred years ago, who came to the conclusion, in the way that scientists are wont to do, that the air at Hindhead was every bit as good as that at Bel Alp, which area he had been in the habit of frequenting for long periods. So, in the 1880s, he built a house 'four square to the winds of heaven' and close to the crossroads which were already well known to travellers on the London to Portsmouth road because of the presence of the Royal Huts Hotel.

Tyndall's enthusiasm for Hindhead soon encouraged other notable people to make the place their home. George Bernard Shaw came to Blen Cathra (now a school), a little way south on the Portsmouth road, and Sir Arthur Conan Doyle built a house (now an hotel) opposite the Royal Huts and called it Undershaw. These great men, and several others, needed staff and gradually Hindhead began to take on the appearance of a village. Shops sprang up around the crossroads and villas were built at Beacon Hill.

Large hotels were built and Hindhead, which had once been a notoriously inhospitable spot, was the 'in' place. Tyndall's home is now flats and surrounded by a council estate which bears his name. The Royal Huts Hotel is, alas, no more, but locals still refer to the place as 'The Huts' in spite of the building's modern role as a motor inn and restaurant.

While modern Hindhead is barely older than this century, there was a settlement in the mid-1800s. The census of 1861 reveals 44 people living there, and with the exception of the innkeeper and, perhaps not surprisingly in view of Cobbett's observations on the place 40 years earlier, a policeman, all the men were either broom makers or agricultural labourers. One family of 12 living in the Devil's Punch Bowl earned their money from three sources. Father and eldest son, aged 15, were broom makers; mother and the two older daughters, aged 19 and 17, were wool spinners; while a 13-year-old son was a shoemaker.

The Devil's Punch Bowl, which is actually in Thursley parish, has been in the care of the National Trust for years. Indeed, much of Hindhead is controlled by the Trust and long may that continue. There is undoubtedly more pollution in the air than in Tyndall's day, but it is still possible to breathe in the freshness of the pines which grow so well on the Greensand. The Punch Bowl was the home of many families whose names can still be found in the area. In the more recent past they were broom makers; earlier they were charcoal burners working in conjunction with the iron masters of the district.

Holmbury St Mary ⁊₰

'This is heaven's gate!' exclaimed the wife of the celebrated Victorian architect George Edward Street, as the couple's carriage brought them to this upland village in 1872. They were on a visit to friends at The Aldermoor on the side of Holmbury Hill, and there and then, it seems, they decided they wanted a house there, too. So they built Holmdale. The village was called Felday in those days and only changed to its present name after Mr Street had designed and paid for a parish church.

G.E. Street, whose London designs include the Law Courts, was clearly a man of considerable standing, and when he died he was buried in Westminster Abbey. In 1880 his home in the village was visited by Gladstone, the prime minister, and the cabinet.

St Mary's which was built in 1879, looks down on the village which nestles around a green with its shops and a pub. It is not hard to imagine it as it was a century and more ago. The area was one of the wildest in the county, and sheep stealers, smugglers and poachers took refuge in the remote hills. Many of the cottages had large cellars where the contraband was hidden.

Holmbury Hill, which Aubrey called a mountain, is, in fact, 857ft above sea level which leaves it short of Hindhead and Leith Hill. There was an early British camp there and Guildford Museum has a collection of artefacts found when the site was excavated in the 1930s.

Holmwood

Wild Holmwood Common was the haunt of highwaymen and smugglers. Now it is owned by the National Trust, thanks to a gift by the Duke of Norfolk in 1956, and altogether a much more hospitable place. The common separates North and South Holmwood, the former is nearer Dorking and suffers as a result of the urban sprawl moving its way.

When James II was the Duke of York the largest stags in England were hunted at Holmwood. Wild boar, too, were pursued to the death, and wild strawberries were plentiful and taken to market by the horse load.

A turnpike road from London to Horsham ran across the common and highway robbers were everywhere. *The Victoria County History* records a man who died in 1902 aged 101 having a workmate who had witnessed a turnpike keeper boldly refusing to open his gate at night to a group of smugglers with kegs of brandy on their horses.

South Holmwood's St Mary Magdalene church was built in 1838 and the site for it, a parsonage and a school, were given by the Duke of Norfolk.

Horne

Hardly a village at all, more a collection of buildings including a church and a school. St Mary's was a chapel of ease to Bletchingley until 1706 but in 1880 it underwent 'pitiful renewal and restoration' say Pevsner and Nairn.

Horsell

There is still something of a village atmosphere about Horsell, in spite of the ever-growing tentacles of Woking, a town which grew with the railway and has consumed so much as resident and businessman have demanded more land for bricks and mortar. But Horsell is just beyond the fringe – at the moment. When the railway first came to the neighbourhood Horsell was so secluded that a place near the canal was selected as a suitable venue for a prize fight. The rich gentlemen came out from London on the train and were conveyed to the ringside which was out of the observation range of the police in Woking.

The church of St Mary is 14th century and stands in a pleasant church yard. Until the turn of the century Horsell comprised a single street surrounded by nurseries. The Cricketers Inn has been used at times as a lock-up, poor house, hospital, school and store. In the mid-19th century a windmill drove a saw pit.

Britain's Muslim community has long been associated with Woking and there was a cemetery on Horsell Common. It was created in 1915 for Indian soldiers who died during the First World War, but after vandalism in the 1950s the bodies were exhumed and buried elsewhere. The Muslim connection with Woking appears to be 100 years old, for it was in 1884 that a Dr Gottlieb Wilhelm Leitner, at one time principal of Punjab University, secured a building in Maybury, a district of Woking, that had been used as a college of drama. A mosque was erected nearer the turn of the century and is still used although the Leitner building has been swallowed by industry.

There were Martians on Horsell Common in 1898, or so H.G. Wells would have us believe in *The War of the Worlds*. Wells lived in Woking for a time and he had the Martians and their machine landing near a sandpit on the common. Wells died in 1946 which was the year the Horsell Common Preservation Society, formed in 1910, obtained a 99-year lease on the 750 acres. The society later secured the freehold.

Horsleys

Like the Clandons to the west, the Horsleys, East and West, are twin villages with many pleasant, rural features. East Horsley, when approached from Guildford, comes upon the traveller in the form of Horsley Towers, a quite unusual building for this part of the country. The present Towers dates from the mid-1800s when most of East Horsley was rebuilt under the direction of the Earl of Lovelace.

Horsley Towers, which has been a training establishment for some years, stands on a sharp bend in the road, which then twists again and heads off for Effingham. East Horsley's church is dedicated to St Martin and there cannot be too many of those around.

West Horsley, for me, is the twin with the charm. It was, it seems, first mentioned in the ninth century and the church of St Mary the Virgin has some pre-Conquest work. Sir Walter Raleigh's head is supposed to be buried in a vault under the south chapel. It was preserved in a red leather bag for 25 years by his widow and then buried along with his son, Carew, who had inherited West Horsley Place in 1643. The claim appears to be substantiated by William Nicholas who, when burying his mother, Penelope, stated there was a head revealed in the vault which was apart from any body or other remains. Penelope Nicholas lost her life when a chimney was brought crashing down onto her bed during the Great Storm of Saturday, November 26, 1703 — the storm which wrecked 15 warships, demolished the Eddystone lighthouse, killed the bishop of Bath and Wells in his palace, and devastated London to the tune of a million pounds.

West Horsley Place has a fascinating history. One of its earlier occupants was Sir James Berners, a follower of Richard II, who was beheaded on Tower Hill in 1388. His daughter was Dame Juliana Berners who part-wrote the *Boke of St Albans* – a 'Treatyse perteynynge to Hawkynge, Huntynge, Fysshynge and Coote Armiris.' A later owner was the Marquis of Exeter who also lost his life on Tower Hill for plotting to murder the King in 1538. And the Earl of Surrey, whose poems about 'Fair Geraldine' were of 13-year-old Elizabeth Fitzgerald, later widow of Sir Anthony Browne of West Horsley Place, lost his head five years after he penned his amorous lines.

Hydestile

There were at one time three hospitals at Hydestile which is a loosely defined area about Hambledon and beyond the outlying station at Milford. King George V Hospital was opened in 1922 by the Metropolitan Asylums Board as a sanatorium for TB patients from London. It had as many as 232 beds in its heyday, but in 1969 its chest work was transferred to Milford Chest Hospital and a unit for mentally handicapped adults was established. The Chest Hospital had been opened in 1928 by the then Minister of Health Mr Neville Chamberlain. The site had been purchased in 1914 but the war interrupted plans and it was not until 11 years later that building commenced. It was originally known as the Surrey County Sanatorium and administered by the county council until 1948. There were 300 beds in six blocks at its peak period. The third hospital to open was Hydestile in 1940, as a hutted annexe to its neighbour, King George V. There are plaques which recall the occupancy of the hospital by members of the 3rd Australian General Hospital in 1940-41 and is a 'tribute to the very gallant part the Commonwealth forces took in the Second World War'. A second plaque bears the arms of St Thomas's Hospital and records: 'St Thomas's Hospital moved here in April 1941 during the bombing of London, leaving behind a casualty and emergency service. After the war, owing to the loss of accommodation through air raids, Hydestile was retained as a branch hospital until March 1968. The governors and staff record their appreciation of the warmth of the local hospitality.' Hydestile hospitals closed at the end of 1985 and the future of the 50 acres of land they occupied is the subject of fierce debate.

The Chest Hospital is on a back road to Godalming which passes through Tuesley where there are some picturesque buildings. In earlier times Minster Field in Tuesley was the site of a church, and a chapel dedicated to the Virgin Mary was in ruins there in 1220. Beyond Hydestile Hospital is Hydon Ball, the 593ft hill which was donated to the National Trust as a memorial to Octavia Hill, a founder of the Trust and a social reformer, who died in 1912. Three years later a party of her friends climbed to the top and watched the unveiling of a granite seat, upon which a plate recorded that it was given in memory of Octavia Hill who was born in 1838.

Hydon Ball is one of a trio of hills in the area, Hascombe and Hambledon are the others, and there is an odd rhyme attached to it, which runs:

On Hydon's top there is a cup
And in that cup there is a drop
Pick up the cup, and drink the drop
And place the cup on Hydon's top

Guildford Museum has a record of a Scottish verse in similar vein, which runs:

On Tinto's top there is a mist
And in the mist there is a kist
And in the kist there is a cup
Take up the cup and drink the drop
And then come down from Tinto's top.

Laleham 🦢

Dr Arnold loved this Thames-side village which came into Surrey from Middlesex in the 1970s. He lived and taught privately here from 1819 to 1828 before moving to the headship of Rugby School and immortality. Thomas Arnold often thought fondly of Laleham as a passage in his biography confirmed: 'Years after he left

Laleham he still retained his early affection for it, and till he had purchased his house in Westmoreland he entertained a lingering hope that he might return to it in his old age, when he retired from Rugby.' Matthew Arnold, the teacher's son who was a poet among other literary things, was born in Laleham in 1822 and was buried in the churchyard of All Saints alongside three brothers who died in childhood. Matthew returned often and once wrote to his mother: 'I was at the old house and under the cedars and by the big pink acacia.' The house was demolished in 1864 and some of the bricks were used to build a school. Laleham Abbey and its 70 acres are in use as a public recreation ground and camping site. It was built in 1803 as Laleham House for the Earl of Lucan who led the Heavy Brigade at Balaclava.

Leigh

This small village near Reigate is where the poet, dramatist and friend of Shakespeare, Ben Jonson, is said to have spent much of his retirement. Leigh, pronounced 'Lye', has an attractive green at its centre with the weatherboarded Plough Inn on one side. Many of the houses are said to be constructed of timbers originally grown in the great oak forests of the district and sawn in earlier times for the manufacture of sailing ships. Whether that is true I do not know; I am no expert, but it is a nice story and fact or legend is, I believe, worth preserving. St Bartholomew's church is small and without aisles, and until 1890 had a timber belfry. That was followed by a stone tower and later a bellcote was added.

Limpsfield

Surrey disappears here where the A25 runs on into Kent. Limpsfield, its common and neighbour Limpsfield Chart nestle below the Downs and are typical east Surrey areas. The main street through Limpsfield runs at right angles to the A25 and is full of half-timbered houses and little nooks and crannies. 'The village street always strikes me as the place swept by eyes of elderly ladies determined to pounce upon any stray piece of paper, eyes that would blaze reproach at the sight of a lump of builders' sand obstructing the pathway,' observed one writer.

The composer Frederick Delius is buried in the churchyard of St Peter's. Born in Yorkshire in 1862, he lived most of his life in France where he died in 1934. He was buried in France but the following year his body was brought back to England and reburied at Limpsfield, where Sir Thomas Beecham, who had been a major influence in bringing the work of Delius to a wider audience, led a torchlight funeral oration. The composer's wife is also buried in the churchyard, as is Harriet Kennard who at the age of 80 nursed men constructing the railway when there was an outbreak of cholera. She, too, died from the disease.

Limpsfield was mentioned in the Domesday Book as being held by the Abbot of Battle. William the Conqueror's surveyors found, among other things, a mill, fishery and church, two stone quarries, and three hawks' nests in the woodland.

Aubrey noted the 'delicate, wholesome and sweet air' of the district, and perhaps this accounted for 12-year-old John Brasie becoming the hero of a cricket match when he made a match-winning score of 84 against local rivals Oxted. The celebrations that followed included a march down the village street led by a brass band lent by the rector.

Lingfield

Racing at Lingfield brings this village in the south-east of the county into public focus, but few of the punters outside of Surrey will be familiar with it. The racecourse was established in 1890 and is to the south of the village in gentle country not far from the borders of Kent and Sussex.

The delight of Lingfield is the church of St Peter and St Paul and its southern approach through a narrow lane of buildings. The church has many memorials to the great Cobham family who lived at nearby Starborough Castle. They fought for King and Country, and Richard, the second Lord Cobham, in his will in 1417, founded

a college close to the church for a provost, six chaplains, four clerks, and 13 poor persons. It remained until 1544 when King Henry VIII had other ideas. The village library is now based in what was the college's guest house.

In the centre of the village is The Cage, once the lock-up. It was last used just over 100 years ago, and in 1850 figured in a dramatic escape when 11 poachers were being held overnight. While the police constable on guard duty dozed off, the poachers' friends stole up under the cover of darkness and removed the roof to free the captives. The Cage is beside a hollow oak and next to the village pond, but the overall setting is of the urban eighties: houses, shops and traffic.

A fascinating little booklet by the late Gordon Jenner, entitled *The Lingfield I Knew*, tells of how one group of villagers was prepared for the start of the First World War. Lt. Lockyer, said Mr Jenner, who lived at Rowlands Court was playing cricket on August 3, 1914, when the local telegraph boy arrived with a message which he handed Lockyer. The officer walked over to his skipper and departed for the pavilion. The other players were told that Lockyer had been recalled to his regiment, and stumps were drawn. The next day war was declared.

Littleton (Guildford) 🌿

A hamlet off the beaten track but only a mile or so from Guildford High Street. But here is Loseley, one of the grandest Elizabethan houses in England. Built with material from the dissolved abbey at Waverley by Sir William More in the 1560s, it continues to be owned by the same family who, through marriage, are now More-Molyneux. There was a west wing which was demolished before the half-way point of the 19th century, and this is believed to have been added around 1600. Loseley, thank goodness, has never become a stately home and therefore the visits that are permitted during the summer months are a joy to make. The estate's dairy farm is well known in the district and visitors can enjoy 'home grown' cream teas.

Littleton is the estate village, well community anyway. There are attractive cottages and the church of St Francis where there was once a school. Littleton Lane, narrow between banks of wild flowers and tall hedges, leads down to the county town but not before it passes a track which affords an access on to the Pilgrims Way and the North Downs Way.

Littleton (Spelthorne) 🌿

There are 7000 million gallons of water on Littleton's doorstep. When Queen Mary Reservoir was opened in 1925 acres of fields, woods and cottages were submerged. It was the largest reservoir of its kind in the world and a breakwater was constructed to restrain the water in high winds. Littleton, which came into Surrey in 1974, was first mentioned in 1042 but did not appear in the Domesday Book because it was attached to Laleham. The manor broke away from Laleham in the 12th century and had a number of owners who lived at Littleton Park until the mansion was burned down in 1974. Since rebuilt it is now a film studio. The building is close to St Mary Magdalene church which has a 13th century chancel and a tower that was built between the 16th and 18th centuries. There is a stained glass window of a painting by Sir John Millais which was given by his widow. Sir John often stayed at the Rectory which was built in 1699.

Lyne ✣

The almoner of Chertsey Abbey lived at Almners Priory in this hamlet to the west of Chertsey where Holy Trinity church is picturesque and early Victorian. The Benedictine abbey of St Peter, Chertsey, was founded in 666 AD. by Erkenwald who subsequently became Bishop of London. The site was marshy and desolate and in the 10th century had to be refounded after the Danes had invaded it. By the Domesday survey in 1068 the abbey owned lands elsewhere in Surrey plus Hampshire and Berkshire. Expansion took place in the 12th century, oak trees were planted, fishponds constructed, and a bridge was built, which is still in use in Guildford Street, Chertsey. The Dissolution came in 1537 and Henry VIII's mason John Nedeham took some of the material for Hampton Court the following year. Excavations have taken place but to all intents and purposes the abbey has been lost for good.

St Ann's Hill which rises to 240 feet is a popular spot with walkers who can see St Paul's Cathedral on a clear day. It was presented to the public in 1928 by Sir William Berry. On the southern slopes was an estate owned by the politician Charles James Fox, and this, too, is open to the public.

Merrow ✣

'There runs a road by Merrow Down – A grassy track today it is – An hour out of Guildford town, Above the river Wey it is.' Merrow Downs were famous long before Kipling wrote those lines. Great horse races took place there, and early cricket matches, too. Now, the Downs are a favourite haunt of ramblers.

Merrow village has taken on the role of Guildford suburb, but the old church of St John the Evangelist which dates from the middle of the 12th century but fell badly into restorers' hands 140 years ago, and the Horse and Groom public house, with a 1615 date on the exterior, stand resolutely amid the new buildings.

There was a public well opposite the inn which was more than 100 feet deep. Buried in the churchyard is one Walter Broke, gent, who died aged 107 in 1603. It is said that when past his 100th birthday he walked from Merrow to London in a day.

But Merrow will always be known for its Downs. The best way to approach them is by foot but for the motorists the old road, up Trodds Lane from the church, is the prettiest. At the summit is Newlands Corner where John St Loe Strachey, proprietor and editor of the *Spectator* for the first quarter of the 20th century, built a house which later became an hotel.

The views are magnificent, as they must have been to the racegoers who flocked to the Downs during Whit week. William III had given a King's Plate of 100 guineas which lapsed under Queen Anne but was renewed by George I. In Victoria's reign it was given as a Queen's Plate. The meeting used to fill Guildford with visitors, but the growth of Epsom and the establishment of Ascot gradually caused a winding down of proceedings. The grandstand was demolished around 1850.

Mr W.C. Smith, in his *Rambles Round Guildford,* 1828, wrote of the Race Downs: 'this place was famous some 20 or 30 years ago for the races held here, and so great was the concourse of people who then visited Guildford, that very exhorbitant sums were not infrequently paid for lodgings and other accommodations during the week.'

Much earlier on Merrow Downs, in 1601, there was a fearful accident during a course of training which left three men dead following a munitions explosion.

Mickleham

This is Fanny Burney country. The daughter of Dr Charles Burney, scholar and musician, who was born in Norfolk in 1752 but established herself as a novelist in Surrey. Fanny wrote *Evelina* while staying at Chessington, and it was this work that made her a force in the literary world. In 1786 she became Second Keeper of the Robes to Queen Charlotte, a position which, it seems, put her under great strain and after five years she was granted retirement. It proved to

be the turning point in her life that she was looking for, and in the following year she met her future husband, the French general, Alexandre Gabriel Jean-Baptiste D'Arblay, whom she married in St Michael's church at Mickleham. Fanny's first meeting with the general was at Juniper Hall, Mickleham, which had become a centre for emigreś from the French Revolution (and is now a National Trust field studies centre). After her marriage, Fanny wrote, among other things, *Camilla* which earned her enough money to build a home at West Humble. They called it Camilla Cottage and today it is remembered by Camilla Lacey, a housing estate in that village.

Milford

The commons to the south of this A3 village were home to thousands of Canadian soldiers during the wars. Now they are nature reserves and conservation areas beloved of walkers and riders. They are in their present conditon because of the care lavished upon them by Ted Chambers who, sadly, died early in 1984. He was responsible for turning overgrown wasteland into something that can now be enjoyed by everyone.

Milford has a station on the London to Portsmouth line half a mile from the village centre, and is soon to have a bypass to bring relief to the heavily congested A3. It is part of the parish of Witley but became a separate ecclesiastical parish 140 years ago when St John's church was built. Almost as old is a firm of plumbers on the original Portsmouth road near the village's crooked crossroads.

The churchyard contains a mausoleum for the Webbs who lived at Milford House, a big, square building dating back to 1730 which became a hotel and has been severely damaged by fire. On the Godalming side of Milford House is the Refectory which was a barn and appears from a sign to claim to be 11th century, before being converted a la Lutyens in the 1930s. Authentic Lutyens can be observed in Rake Manor near the station which was an original early 17th century building.

The A3 swings past Moushill Green which is worth more than a glance. Here are some attractive old cottages leading down to the Heath where cricket has been played since 1816. In that area until recently was the non-conformist chapel which had its roots in Milford in a building which had been, appropriately, a cattle shed. Some of the shed was used in the construction of the first chapel in 1860 and there was a room for 60 people. Twelve years later an iron chapel was secured from Alton and at a total cost of £742 a new site and building afforded room for 150 worshippers and, in an adjoining schoolroom, 60 children.

Congregationalism continued to grow in the village and in 1902 the iron building was dwarfed by a new stone chapel which accommodated 200 people and cost £1200. Milford, and its neighbour at Elstead, enjoyed happy times, but slowly attendances declined and now only Elstead remains, while Milford's needs are looked after by Godalming.

Moleseys 🦢

These riverside urban areas face Hampton Court across the Thames which in Henry VIII's time was crossed by ferry. A wooden bridge went up in 1753 and was replaced by another structure of wood 25 years later. In 1865 the river was spanned by iron and then, in 1933, Lutyens and W.P. Robinson, an engineer, built the present Hampton Court bridge. East Molesey was linked to the capital by train in February 1849 and this transformed the district, fields and orchards disappearing in favour of houses.

West Molesey has long had a sporting side. At Molesey Hurst archery, cricket, horse racing, golf, barefist boxing and even illicit duelling have drawn large crowds. Cricket was recorded there as early as 1731 and it is held that the first leg before wicket decision was recorded there in 1775. In 1758 there was one of the country's earliest golf matches and in the early 1800s large bets were placed as prize fighters slugged it out for hours at a time. More recently Hurst Park racecourse was a popular venue for punters who came out from London. The course was laid in 1890 and lasted until 1962 when it was sold for housing development. Molesey's football ground at the Priory was the scene of an early balloon ascent in May 1785.

Munstead 🦢

Gertrude Jekyll is everywhere in west Surrey, but her presence is probably greatest here in this leafy appendage south of Godalming. Munstead House was built for her and her mother on open heath by J. J. Stevenson in 1877–8, and when Mrs Jekyll died in 1895 her son, Sir Herbert, took over the house, with Gertrude moving to Munstead Wood which Edwin Lutyens built for her. Earlier, when Mrs Jekyll was alive, Gertrude had commissioned Lutyens to build The Hut so that she could receive her friends.

Lutyens and Jekyll in west Surrey go together like milk and cream, the great gardener adding the topping to the fine designs. Lutyens was born in Thursley in 1869, knighted in 1918, and died in 1944. His architecture is universally known. He set up a London practice at the age of 19 and was consulting architect for the Hampstead Garden Suburb project in 1908, the joint architect for the building of New Delhi from 1913, designer of the Cenotaph in Whitehill in 1919, plus buildings such as the British Embassy in Washington, the Midland Bank in the City, and Grosvenor House in Park Lane. The Second World War prevented his designs for a Roman Catholic cathedral in Liverpool coming to fruition.

Gertrude Jekyll, who was born in 1843, lived at Munstead Wood for 35 years. She had to forsake her first love of painting when her eyesight deteriorated, but this personal loss quickly became the gain of horticulturalists everywhere. Miss Jekyll encouraged the younger Lutyens in his work, and her skill was the perfect complement.

Munstead lies in the area of Winkworth Arboretum, and was in recent years a base for the late Shah of Persia who owned Stilemans, but there is no record of the ruler of the Peacock Throne ever coming to Munstead.

Newdigate ❧

This quiet, sleepy village down near the Sussex border was the first place in the county to have an iron works. It was in 1553 at Ewood to the north of the village that Christopher Darrell set up his foundry and was able to make use of a directive which allowed him to use trees on his land, whereas Elizabethan Acts prevented others from felling timber 'for making coles for the making of iron.'

There has always been a good quantity of wood around Newdigate, and many of the older houses have local oak in their construction. St Peter's church probably dates from the 13th century, and its dominant feature is its wooden tower and octagonal spire. The tower is supported by oak beams and, with the one at Burstow, is the only all-wooden tower in the county.

The tower contains six bells 'of whose silvery notes the Newdigate men are justly proud', said an earlier writer. Bellringers from the village have been well known for decades. The Old Six Bells was a smugglers' haunt with underground passages, one of which was said to lead to the vicarage.

An early parson was George Steere, who was appointed by King James in 1610, and who gave a school house and £6 13s 4d a year to teach four children. The school was in ruins in 1838 and a new building erected in 1872.

Normandy ✣

Cobbett died here in 1835. The great politician spent his last days at Normandy Farm, but his body was taken back the few miles to Farnham, his birthplace, and buried in the family grave close to the main door of St Andrew's church in the town.

William Cobbett was born in Bridge Square, Farnham, at the public house which now bears his name, in 1762. He is best remembered for his *Rural Rides*, a collection of writings about his horseback journeys, many of them through Surrey. But Cobbett was also variously a gardener, lawyer's clerk, soldier, politician and farmer. He even served two years in jail for seditious libel for which he was also fined £1000.

Guildford Races came to Normandy in the 1870s, long after the halcyon days of the turf on Merrow Downs and following an experiment on a track at Chilworth. But the event got a bad press in the *Surrey Advertiser* in an editorial under the heading: The Perils of Sporting in Surrey. 'Greece may be bad, but really Normandy (in England, we mean) on Monday was worse, for gentlemen who went there fancied that no military escort would be required,' ran the piece.

'They were sadly mistaken. Quietly pinioned in open daylight, in the sight of hundreds, they were relieved of valuable field glasses, or within a stone's throw of a railway station, held while watches and money were stolen, the bandits with cool assurance, saying that these were somewhat of the kind of thing they required.'

The editorial mentioned 'plunder, gambling and rowdyism' at Normandy but ended by stating that 'racing is a perfectly lawful sport, that it is patronised by the highest personages in the land, and that so long as it occupies this position, those who take part in it ought to have that protection which the law guarantees to all persons in this country who may be engaged in lawful pursuits.'

On the same page of the newspaper was a letter from someone who signed himself 'Promoter'. It claimed that the Chief of the County Constabulary was 'neglect' as he was 'informed at Scotland Yard that the County men were bound to protect the public. I am indeed sorry to hear so many gentlemen were robbed.'

Pigs were a problem for users of the commons back in the 1920s. They obstructed the footpaths and made them dirty, and parish councillors won permission from the War Office to erect stiles and gates to stop animals from leaving the commons, although the paths remained unfenced. There had been swine in the area since time immemorial, on land from which Henley Park evolved. Henley Park, a mansion built in the 1700s, was the headquarters of an engineering concern until 1983 when it was sold.

Norney

St Mary's Church which stands at the crossroads at Norney is the work of the eminent architect, Sir George Scott. It is the parish church of Shackleford but is isolated from the centre of the village and, as part of a team ministry, appears to be used less frequently than in years gone by. Scott, the architect, was the son of a Buckinghamshire clergyman, and was born in 1811. His commissions, with his partner, William Bonython Moffatt, were thought to number at least 750, and included the Albert Memorial in Kensington Gardens, the Martyrs' Memorial at Oxford, Reading Gaol, the entrance to Dean's Yard at Westminster, restoration at Bath Abbey, the Home Office and Foreign Office in Whitehall, and St Pancras Station Hotel. So Shackleford's parish church, and several others in the county, were the creation of an architect whose work is known to everyone who visits the capital.

Sir George died in 1878 and his sons maintained the family's eminence. George Gilbert, the younger (1837 - 97), who was the eldest son, and John Oldrid (1841 - 1913), the second son, carved themselves a reputation in the field of architecture. George Gilbert was a Fellow of Jesus College, Cambridge, where he had an academic career of distinction. He was later in a partnership which produced church fittings of pre-Raphaelite design, and assisted his father and brother. He was the author in 1884 of the *History of English Church Architecture*, and editor of his father's book, *Personal and Professional Recollections.*

George Gilbert's second son, Giles Gilbert, who was knighted in the 1920s, won a competition in 1903 for the design of the Anglican Cathedral in Liverpool, and when he died in 1960 it was still to be completed. Locally, Sir Giles Gilbert Scott designed the War Memorial Chapel at Charterhouse School, Godalming, and in London his works included Battersea Power Station, Waterloo Bridge, and the rebuilding of the House of Commons.

The church at Norney is a mile from the centre of Shackleford village, but this little area just off the A3 has a community feel about it, no doubt brought on by the presence of the village hall and the junior school, a mellow Victorian building which gives the appearance of being a pleasant place to learn one's elementary education, a contention supported, perhaps, by the standard of work displayed at exhibitions, including the annual Surrey County Show. The children at the 1984 show had the honour of singing for Princess Anne.

The lych gate at the church is to the memory of William Brodrick, the eighth Viscount Midleton of nearby Peper Harow, and on the war memorial on the opposite side of the road are the names of 24 men from Shackleford and Peper Harow who were killed in the First World War, and a further five, including Major the Hon. M.V. Brodrick, MC, Coldstream Guards, who did not return from the 1939-45 hostilities.

Phyllis Nicholson, an authoress, loved Norney during the 1930s and 1940s and wrote about the beauty of the place. It remains a rural corner in spite of the rush of traffic close by.

Nutfield

There is an industry as old as the Romans in this A25 village east of Redhill. The history of the village is bound up in the gathering of fuller's earth at sites to the north of the main road. Fuller's earth was first recorded in the Roman period and over the centuries has sustained many a Nutfield family.

Its original use was in the preparation of woollen and worsted cloth, and was therefore in great demand in the south-west of the county in the 15th, 16th and 17th centuries. Now, its properties have a wider application, such as in refining oil and in toilet preparations, and the earth is exported around the world. That was not the case in the reign of Edward II when export of the substance was prohibited.

The Domesday survey noted a church and a mill in Nutfield, but the present church dates from the 12th century. There were mills north and south of the village, and the southern one, King's Mill, was featured in a documentary film some years ago entitled 'One hundred years of gearing'.

Four hundred years ago conditions were so tough that one man was given leave to attend a church other than Nutfield's because travelling was so difficult that he could not be at morning service, return home and be back for evening prayers as he was required to do. Permission was granted provided that the man attended Nutfield church four times a year to take Communion.

In Elizabeth I's time Martin Gummyns, a collier, of Nutfield, was sentenced to be hanged for burglary. He and others unknown stole a pair of sheets (worth 6s 8d), two shirts (6s), a smock (3s 4d), a cupboard cloth (6s), five rails (10s), five kerchiefs (5s), and two ells of holland cloth (4s), and Gummyns was sentenced at Croydon Assizes in 1579.

Ockham

Nestling quietly to the east of the new A3 and south of London's southern bypass, the M25, Ockham has long been dominated by its park which was bought by the first Lord King who was Queen Anne's Lord Chancellor. It eventually passed into the hands of his descendants, the Lovelaces, whose name is used to indicate the local ward on Guildford Borough Council.

The old semaphore station on Chatley Heath, near the village, is a monument now; 150 years ago it was a vital link in the chain which sent messages to and from the Admiralty in London to ships in the Channel. Chatley Heath was the point at which the unfinished branch line to Plymouth set off for Worplesdon, the Hog's Back and beyond. In those days wells on the local commons yielded deposits of Epsom salt.

This was the birthplace of William de Ockham who, before he died in 1349, engaged in controversies with Popes John XXII and Benedict XII.

In the churchyard, noted Manning and Bray, was the body of a very large oak, 12ft high and with the top broken off, and in the middle was a young oak. Also in the churchyard, a gravestone to a carpenter named Spong had a verse composed by Lord King the Lord Chancellor which went:

'Who many a sturdy oak had laid along,
Fell'd by death's surer hatchet, here lies Spong.
Posts oft he made, yet ne'er a place could get,
And liv'd by railing, tho' he was no wit.
Old saws he had, altho' no antiquarian;
And styles corrected, yet was no grammarian.
Long liv'd he Ockham's premier architect;
And lasting as his fame a tomb t'erect
In vain we seek an artist such as he,
Whose pales and gates were for eternity.
So here he rests from all life's toils and follies,
O spare awhile, kind Heav'n, his fellow labourer Hollis!'

Hollis was said to be the estate bricklayer.

Ockley 🌺

There are red roses around some of the gravestones in St Margaret's churchyard – just as there were 300 years ago when that great rambler, John Aubrey, came upon Ockley. 'Anciently the custom here for betrothed lovers was to plant rose trees at the head of the grave of a deceased lover, should either party die before the wedding. In the churchyard are many red rose trees planted among the graves which have been there beyond man's memory,' wrote Aubrey in the 17th century.

C. Howkins
'98-9

105

Today's roses are not the ones Aubrey saw, but there is the impression that little has changed in this corner of the parish. The village of Ockley lies on a straight section of the A29 and it is not surprising to discover that here was the road the Romans knew as Stone or Stane Street. It is as straight as a die, and through travellers are forced to miss the beauty of the place because of the constant speed the road affords.

There are four pubs along the road through the village and many old timbered cottages look out onto the cricket field on Ockley Green. Sportsmen have done battle for years alongside the A29, but go back more than 11 centuries and there was a battle of a different kind on Ockley Green and up the slopes of nearby Leith Hill. In 851, more than 200 years before the Battle of Hastings, the Danes were routed. The invaders swept through Kent and down the Thames. Their target was Winchester, but they had not reckoned with Ethelwulf of Wessex. He marched up Stone Street from Chichester and faced the enemy 'hard by Ockley wood'. The battle was fierce and at the end there were few Danes left to tell the tale. 'Blood stood ankle deep' after the slaughter.

Old Woking

This was the original Woking and in the 17th century a market town. Henry VIII knew it for its Old Palace, as did Elizabeth I and James I, the latter giving Edward Zouch of Hoe Place the manor in 1620. Zouch was responsible for demolishing the palace whose materials were spread around with the stained glass ending up at Sutton Place. In the grounds of Hoe Place was a brick tower from which a beacon was said to direct messengers to James I when he was staying with Zouch. However, a letter in the *Surrey Advertiser* in 1926 from Lord Onslow stated that the tower stood on land once owned by his father. His lordship understood the tower had been used as a beacon or telegraph station for naval signalling between London and Portsmouth, and that it was supposed to have been used in the fight against the Spanish Armada.

Onslow Village 🦢

One mile from Guildford's famous High Street setts, and looked down on by the cathedral, is this planned village which was established in the 1920s on land owned by Lord Onslow, grandfather of the present earl who lives at Clandon Park. The Onslow Village Association bought the land and over the years it kept a tight rein on the development of the area. In 1984, though, feelings were aroused and headlines made when the association, in the face of Government policy on home ownership and tenants' rights to buy, decided to dissolve and offered the shareholding tenants their homes at considerably less than the market value.

Ottershaw 🦢

Sir Gilbert Scott's red-brick Christ Church is a striking feature of this widespread village built on the heath between Woking and Chertsey. Built in 1864, it stands on a knoll beside the main road with the rounded altar end in striking contrast to the spire. Ottershaw does not appear in the Domesday Book but long before the survey King Alfred's charter of 890 referred to land called Otreshagh which is thought to be at this place.

Thomas Day, an 18th century writer of children's literature, lived at Anningsley Park and according to a writer at the turn of the century he was a man 'whose life and character occupy an extremely interesting chapter in the records of the eccentricities of genius'. In the last eight years of his life from 1781 he 'took up farming energetically, lived simply without a carriage, saw no society, and spent his income upon improving his estate. He lost money by his farm, but was consoled by the employment given to the poor. He declined invitations to take part in political agitation, preferring his schemes of moral and social reform, and approving of Pitt's administration. He studied mechanics, chemistry, and physic, became a good lawyer, and wrote *Sandford and Merton* to set forth his ideal of manliness.'

Outwood 🌿

There will always be a steady stream of visitors to this hamlet because of its windmill. The place is off the beaten track but there is some good country round about, and the tiny cricket ground is picturesque. But it is the windmill which people come to see.

Those who went there before November 1960 saw two mills. Now the post mill stands alone on its lofty site. It is said to be the oldest working mill in England, having been built in 1665-66 when, the story goes, the men working on it watched London burn.

The larger of the two mills, known as a smock mill because its shape resembled that of an old countryman's smock, collapsed of old age almost a quarter of a century ago.

Oxshott ༄

Commuter land amid heaths, close to A3 and M25, railway station to Waterloo, pleasant towns of Leatherhead and Esher close by. Not the words of an estate agent but my description of Oxshott. Luxury homes abound in this urban village with its busy shopping centre. It has been known as Oakshott, Ockshot and Oxshot, and in its High Street around 1913 were found five sherds of Roman pottery. Bottles of Jessops Wells water at 6d each were said to contain a powerful potion from a well in woods near Fairoak Lane, Oxshott.

Oxted ༄

The old village is a charming place but all around there has been development. The A25 runs through the shopping centre and away from Barrow Green Court, the manor house, which is 17th century and once the home of the historian Grote. Close by is St Mary's church with its short 12th century tower. The Old Bell Inn is 15th century and a well known watering hole in East Surrey. Oxted's Master Park was a gift by Charles Hoskins Master, lord of the manor, who in 1923 decreed that 'the greater part of the Marls Field as it is originally known laid out and preserved for ever thereafter for the healthy recreation and amusement of the inhabitants of the parish of Oxted and their friends'.

Peaslake ❧

This is one of the county's most out of the way villages, tucked away on the slopes of Hurt Wood which was given to the public for 'air and exercise' in the 1920s. The Bray family of Shere, in whose parish Peaslake is situated, has quarried the local hillside for generations, and there are many properties built of Pitch Hill stone.

The church of St Mark was constructed of local sandstone and much of the carving was done by village craftsmen. It celebrated its centenary in 1989. The Romans were in Peaslake in the second century; the late Sir Adrian Boult had a home in the village in recent years; and there is a last resting place for Quakers in a special burial ground.

There is some fine walking and riding country and many visitors quench their thirst at the accommodating Hurtwood Inn.

Peasmarsh ❧

A grizzly past is attached to this area in the parish of Shalford between Guildford and Godalming, for it was the place where public hangings were carried out. One, about 1820, saw men on the gallows after the murder of a farmer and theft of a side of bacon. One is said to have called to the other: 'Shall I? Shall I?' This was thought to mean 'Shall I confess?' The other replied: 'No. Damn it, die like a man.'

Peasmarsh today comprises little more than a few houses, some industry and a crematorium. It lies between the river Wey and the main railway line between London and Portsmouth. A busy road with two congested junctions makes it a place to avoid at peak periods.

It is not the place Cobbett would remember travelling through in 1882. 'Everybody that has been from Godalming to Guildford,' he wrote, 'knows that there is hardly another such a pretty four miles in all England. The road is good; the soil is good; the houses are neat; the people are neat; the hills, the woods, the meadows, all are beautiful. Nothing wild and bold, to be sure; but exceedingly pretty, and it is almost impossible to ride along these four miles without feelings of pleasure, though you have rain for your companion, as it happened to be with me.'

Peasmarsh is still tolerably rural and the main cluster of houses are separated from the road by a wide expanse of common land. In the early years of this century children swarmed to Peasmarsh Common to climb trees and watch the delivery carts being driven through the ponds to keep the wheels moist and prevent the nails from falling out. It is recorded a red-backed shrike once nested there. This is the now rare bird known as the butcher because it impales its prey on thorns or barbed wire. Perhaps its nesting location was apt in view of Peasmarsh's past association.

Peper Harow ꧁

Peper Harow Park was the seat of the Lords Midleton of Cork from the early 1700s. Now, the mansion is a school. The Midletons have left but the park remains much as it was. The present house was built in 1775, south-east of the original one which was where the second Duke of Richmond (of Goodwood) was entertained while playing Alan Brodrick (Lord Midleton's son and heir) at cricket.

The ground on which they played is used today by the Peper Harow Cricket Club, and the 18th century gentlemen led their teams in games played to rules which were, in part, not dissimilar to our Laws of Cricket. On a visit to the park, and with but a touch of imagination, you can picture the scene. The rustic quality remains, albeit under the care of more modern machinery. There, too, are the Cedars of Lebanon which were planted as seedlings from pots in 1735.

Peper Harow appeared in Domesday Book and the mill in 1086 could have been at Eashing just a little way downstream on the Wey. There are bridges almost as old in the park and, like others in the neighbourhood, seem certain to have been constructed by the Cistercian monks from Waverley. On the edge of the parish is a popular riverside spot called Somerset Bridge. Again the Wey is crossed by a fine bridge, the middle arch being 700 years old, and it is on the site of the Saxon river crossing of Sumoeres forda. The highways authorities have, to their credit, refrained from adding an accompanying bridge as has happened elsewhere, notably upstream at Elstead and Tilford.

The Waverley monks farmed at Oxenford on the edge of Peper Harow Park on land that had been granted to their abbey in the early 12th century. The buildings at Oxenford are imitation 13th century. The fifth viscount employed Pugin to build a farm and gatehouse in 1844 in a style which bore resemblance to the grange which had been pulled down 69 years earlier. That leaves the pond close to the road as the most ancient relic at Oxenford.

Pugin also built an arch in the same style over nearby Bonfield Spring which, said Aubrey, cured sore eyes and ulcers. The perambulator also noted that 'near to this place, by digging for carrots (two spits deep) have been found gold and silver money, not Roman, but old English; as also rings ...; which makes the inhabitants give 2s per acre more than elsewhere, in hopes of finding more.'

Graves of the Midletons are in the churchyard of St Nicholas near to the mansion. The little church was worked on by Pugin after one of its incumbents, the Rev. Owen Manning, had become known as the compiler of much of a major history of the county. A much later vicar, the Rev. William Shaw, was a noted natural historian who observed in 1925 that a thorn tree at the end of the church was 800 years old, and yew trees in the churchyard were 1300 years old and would live as long again.

Pirbright ✺

The heart of this attractive village is very green. There is a lot of open space in the centre where sport is played and children play. The village duck pond is overlooked by shops and the Cricketers pub which has an attractive sign depicting a scene from the game as it looked in the 18th century.

Pirbright is not entirely surrounded by military land but a large chunk of it is, and the two appear to get on. One suspects that the villagers have learned to live with the Army, so long have the soldiers been around. In 1911 it was recorded that three-quarters of the parish had been acquired by the War Office.

Church Lane leads not unnaturally to St Michael's which has a square, rather squat tower made, said one writer in the last century, with 'stones dug from the neighbouring commons'. The churchyard stretches back towards the village, and just inside the gate is the grave of Henry Morton Stanley, the man who uttered the immortal words: 'Dr Livingstone, I presume.' Stanley, an American journalist, talked his way into the history books in 1871 when, having been sent to Africa to look for Livingstone, he met the Scottish explorer beside Lake Tanganyika. Stanley was then 30 years old and he lived for another 33 years. He had requested that his body be buried beside that of Livingstone in Westminster Abbey but this was refused, and so his last resting place became a Surrey churchyard beneath a huge piece of Dartmoor granite – a British menhir, one writer called it – which dwarfs all the other memorials.

Back in 1802 Pirbright's vestry received the sum of two shillings and sixpence from George III as a token of his majesty's gratitude after villagers had rescued him from a bog when his coach overturned on the outskirts of the settlement. Earlier still Pirbright had been the home of Admiral John Byron, an explorer and grandfather of the poet, who planted an avenue of Scots firs called Admiral's Walk which extended for a mile over Government land attached to the ranges.

A drinking fountain in the village was given by Lord and Lady Pirbright to mark Queen Victoria's diamond jubilee in 1897; they also gave the village hall, in 1899, and the recreation ground which was completed in 1901 as a memorial to Edward VII's accession.

Pixham

A Lutyens church and a mill are two delights in this area north-east of Dorking. St Martin's church was built in 1903 while the earliest date known for a mill at Pixham is 1595 although the present mill has a 1837 date. When it was put up for sale a century ago it was advertised as 'situate on a stream of water that never fails'. This was the Pippbrook which rises on Leith Hill and flows a few miles to enter the Mole at Pixham. The mill was working until the mid-1920s and is now a private residence.

Puttenham

There is an inscription on a gravestone in the cemetery which reads: 'In their deaths they were not divided.' A quite ordinary line, perhaps, but in the case of Albert and Annie Keen there is an extraordinary story. These two country folk were the victims of a brutal double murder, and their killer was never brought to justice.

The Keens lived in a simple cottage which bore their name on common land in the south of the parish. They had lived there since their marriage, and Albert was born there. His family had been the occupants for more than one hundred years. Their lives had been quite unspectacular. Albert had worked for several of the big houses round about, and was a farm foreman at the time of his death.

They died in October 1932; Annie in the scullery of their home, and Albert on the way home, his body being found in nearby Cutt Mill Pond. A massive police operation led to the arrest of a man with local connections, but after a trial at Surrey Assizes at Kingston he was acquitted.

Albert and Annie Keen were buried in a grave next to his parents', and more than 50 years later their story is remembered only by older residents of the district.

The ponds at Cutt Mill are hauntingly beautiful. Six in all, they are known by their collective name but accurately should be referred to as Cutt Mill Pond, The Tarn, Warren Pond, General's Pond, Long Pond, and Trout Pond. The Tarn is the one beloved of walkers and anglers.

Puttenham's church nestles at one end of the village street, and there was once a spire on top of the tower, but this was destroyed by a fire in 1736 which started in the blacksmith's forge. Water for the village was taken from a well just inside the church gate until the mid-1700s when the source was filled in. Then, on Palm Sunday in 1972, churchgoers were surprised to see a very pleasant cypress tree drop through the ground. The village well, which few knew about, had reappeared. Behind the church is Puttenham Priory, a large residence which was once owned by the founder of *Picture Post* magazine. Built in 1762, the Priory was bought from Sir Edward Hulton by Guildford Hospital Management Committee in 1950 and, for 26 years until it was sold, was an old people's home.

Henry Beedell and his son, also Henry, were successive rectors for 96 years, while another Puttenham priest was Charles Kerry whose work as an archaeologist and local historian is still referred to. The Kerry manuscripts record many interesting stories, including a nice piece of folk lore about the siting of the church in Puttenham. According to Kerry's papers the church was to be sited on Church Croft Knob in a plantation well out of the village on the way to Cutt Mill. But the pious intentions of the builders, Kerry was told, were frustrated by fairies who removed by night what had been erected in the day to the place were the church now stands. Church Croft continues to appear on maps.

Puttenham, sheltered on the south side of the Hog's Back, is a popular village close enough to the county town for convenience but still with a rural identity. Its golf course stretches over the heath where Queen Victoria reviewed the Surrey Rifle Volunteers in 1851. Puttenham was until quite recently the eastern limit of the Alton and Farnham hop fields, and was, on Bowen's map of 1749, 'noted for its pleasant and healthy situation.' Bowen, two centuries on, could probably make that claim today.

Pyrford

The old church of St Nicholas looks across to the ruined Newark Priory from its position above the Wey, but since 1966 there is no longer a view of Newark Mill. The building, said Mr J. Hillier in his 1950s book, *Old Surrey Water-mills*, must take pride of place among such structures in Surrey. It was one of the few generally known outside Surrey. Sadly, it was burned down 18 years ago.

Elizabeth I was a visitor to Pyrford when a secretary, Sir John Wolley, and his wife, who was a member of the More family of Loseley and a lady-in-waiting to the queen, lived at Pyrford Place. The estate was bought by Denzil Onslow in 1677 but the house was demolished 100 years later by Robert Onslow. John Aubrey has left us with the following record of a visit on August 23, 1681: '... there was much company, and such an extraordinary feast, as I had hardly seen at any country gentleman's table. What made it more remarkable was that there was not anything save what his (Denzil

By
Pyrford Lock
29-10-1982

Onslow) estate about it affords; as venison, rabbits, hares, pheasants, partridges, pigeons, quails, poultry, all sorts of fowl in season from his own decoy near his house, and all sorts of fresh fish. After dinner, we went to see sport at the decoy, where I never saw so many herons. The seat stands in a flat, the ground pasture rarely watered and exceedingly improved since Mr Onslow bought it. The house is timber, but commodious, with one ample dining room.'

The parish shares its living with Wisley and has been known as Pyrford-cum-Wisley. The incumbent through both World Wars was the Rev. Cuthbert Hamilton who moved from Farnham, where he had been a curate for three years, in 1913. Mr Hamilton was a regular member of Farnham's cricket team and a more than useful batsman.

Ripley

Cricket and cycling made Ripley famous in the 19th century. One took place on the Green behind the main road, the other centred around the gabled and low ceilinged Anchor Inn. Ripley, 25 miles from the centre of London before modern roads shrunk the distance, was the ideal halfway stop for early cyclists as the sport began to take a hold in the south.

The first riders came to the village in 1870 and the Dibble sisters, Annie and Harriet, welcomed them to their hostelry. They made such a fuss of them that in any one year almost 7000 cyclists, mounted on penny-farthings or boneshakers, signed the visitors' book at the Anchor where Annie Dibble, like her sister, a devout churchgoer, was known to read the Bible to her guests.

When these two ladies died – Annie in July 1895 and Harriet in October the following year – cyclists clubbed together and had a stained glass window in memory installed in the south aisle of St Mary's church in the village.

Ripley cricketers have been active for more than two centuries. In 1749 they combined with players from Richmond to play London, and two years later they joined forces with Thursley cricketers to meet the Gentlemen of Eton. Ripley Green was the venue of a match between Chertsey and the rest of Surrey in 1762 when an ordinary (meal) was supplied by Mr Fowler's White Horse. Surrey played Middlesex there in 1763; and 22 of Surrey challenged England at Ripley in 1802. The village also joined with Cobham, Woking and Pirbright to play two matches against the five-year-old Farnham club in 1787. Farnham were asked to exclude their best bowler in the first fixture, in spite of the already unbalanced nature of the side, but still won by seven wickets. The return, at Ripley went to the home side by 101 runs.

Cricket is still played in the village, and cyclists continue to call but the days of the Dibbles are long gone. Ripley High Street, alas, has been choked by traffic for too many years, in spite of a bypass being constructed, but the Anchor and the Talbot Hotel, where Nelson often stopped, continue to be popular hostelries.

Rowledge

The parish church of St James in Rowledge is in Hampshire. So, too, is the village school. A big hitter on the cricket field can hit the ball into the next county. The church is on the edge of Alice Holt Forest, which is wholly in Hampshire and has provided Rowledge men with work over the centuries.

Rowledge has grown considerably in recent years but still retains some village charm. The square with its shops and public house, the Hare and Hounds, has always been a meeting place. Nearby, High Street gives the impression of hustle and bustle but it is just a residential road which once contained some handy shops.

Surrey ends and Hampshire begins in Fuller's Road which takes its name from one Nestor Fuller who, more than one hundred years ago, came to Frensham Hill, a large house on the outskirts of the village and now renamed Frensham Heights School. The brewing family Charrington occupied Frensham Hill in the early part of this century and the beautiful cricket ground in front of the house was the scene of some memorable matches. Cricket week at Frensham Hill was an annual occasion not to be missed, and local folk helped cater for such famous teams as MCC, Free Foresters and I Zingari.

There has always been a strong cricket tradition in Rowledge and district. Just outside the village, in Hampshire, is the hamlet of Holt Pound where Surrey twice defeated England in the early 1800s. Rowledge cricketers used that same oval – the name was taken up by Surrey County Cricket Club when it moved to Kennington in 1845 – until their recreation ground was prepared.

The village club dominated the local I'Anson Cup league earlier in the 1980s, before leaving for pastures new. In 1985 it became the village champions of England, and played at Lord's where it lost a nail-biting final to the Scottish champions.

Mike Hawthorn, Britain's first world motor racing champion, lived in Rowledge and was a colourful character in the district. Hawthorn, who won the title in 1958, lived life to the full but it lasted just short of 30 years, for the dashing bow-tied driver died at the wheel of a Jaguar in an accident on the Guildford bypass on January 22, 1959. He was a boyhood hero and I well remember him telling at an assembly at Farnham Grammar School shortly before he died how he had won the world championship. His funeral service and procession stopped Farnham in its tracks and the wreaths and floral tributes at his graveside were from the legends and the elite of world motor racing. His gravestone in the town's cemetery depicts a racing car surrounded by a laurel wreath under which is the inscription 'A gay gallant sportsman'. Hawthorn's TT garage in East Street, Farnham, was a mecca for boys who would press their noses against the plate glass and look at the gleaming racing cars and, hopefully, catch a glimpse of their idol. His death was a stunning blow to boys of my age who were beginning to tinker with old cars, and as keenly felt as the air crash at Munich the previous year which had robbed us of our favourite 'Busby Babes'.

Runfold

When driving along the A31 at Runfold you barely notice a property called Barfield. It is a school and lies back off the road on the junction of the lane to Crooksbury Hill. The motorist does not have time to look anywhere but ahead at this particular point. Few drivers would know of the significance of that spot, anyway. The name of John Henry Knight means little to most passers by. But to those who know their motoring history J.H. Knight is recalled as a pioneer. Five years before the dawn of this century Knight invented the first two-seater car and it was made in nearby Farnham.

Knight lived at Barfield, and the dusty, rutted roads round about were his test bed. He and his machines were a familiar sight in the district, preceded by a man carrying a red flag. His 1895 invention was capable of eight miles an hour and put the life of the flag carrier in peril, and at least on one occasion earned Knight a fine in the local magistrates' court.

Farnham was, and still is, rightly proud of him, and present-day Runfold has, it seems, been content to let its big brother have the glory.

Runfold, once in the centre of hop fields, is now a place to be passed through with barely a sideways glance, but to the south there is some delightful country dominated by Crooksbury Hill, first topped by pine trees more than 200 years ago. Those conifers have been a landmark for generations, in spite of being decimated during the Great War, but now a flight direction beacon stands out more prominently on the skyline, albeit on an adjoining hill.

On its southern slopes is Crooksbury House which was Lutyens' first country house in 1890. He designed it for Arthur Chapman and within a few years he was enlarging it. There was additional work in the early years of this century when Gertrude Jekyll added her influence in the garden.

Rushmoor

This is an outpost of the civil parish of Frensham and ecclesiastical parish of Churt and lies between Hankley and Churt commons. The road through Rushmoor is known locally as the 'Straight Mile' and it leads to the Pride of the Valley (see Churt) which offers comfortable accommodation but was once a most rural of wayside public houses.

Across the road from the inn a path leads to the top of one of three conical hills known as the Devil's Jumps. The other two are private property, but Stony Jump is owned by the National Trust and affords a panoramic view through 360 degrees. The large outcrop of sandstone gives the hill its name but how did the Jumps become linked with the devil? Two legends have stood the test of time. One has the devil leaping from hill to hill while fleeing from Mother Ludlam at Waverley, coming to rest on nearby Kettlebury Hill before disappearing into Heccombe Bottom which is known now as the Devil's Punch Bowl. The other has the devil jumping from hill to hill and being knocked out with a stone thrown by Thor the god of thunder whose name is perpetuated in the neighbouring village of Thursley.

The Devil's Jumps have even been discussed in the House of Lords. In the 1920s their lordships were critical of the way the heather was being burnt and replaced with trees. Sheer vandalism, they claimed, but the Forestry Commission reported that it was providing jobs in a depressed area and, anyway, when the trees matured the beauty of the area would be enhanced. How right it was, but you have got to stand on the top of Stony Jump to agree. Try it at sunset on a summer's day or, if you want exhilaration, be there when a wind is blowing.

Salfords

A 'sad example of ribbon development' is one comment levelled at this village on the A23 south of Redhill. It is a fair description. Salfords, years ago, was quite rural, but the developers, both domestic and industrial, moved in and changed the face of the place. The parish council boundary takes in Sidlow to the west and here there is still green countryside. The Sal brook runs through Salfords and enters the Mole near Sidlow; once it supplied water for a mill which twice burnt down before being converted into a guest house to cater for the demand brought about by the increase of traffic on the main road to Brighton on which, until 1881, there was a toll bridge. Salfords church of Christ the King is modern and was built by voluntary labour.

Seale

The roof tops of Seale can just be spotted through the trees on the drive over the Hog's Back between Farnham and Guildford. North of the ridge is the urban sprawl of Aldershot and district, while south, which is where Seale lies, is rural, agricultural land, pockmarked here and there with gravel pits.

Seale has lost its shop and post office and its small school is under threat, but it has pleasant old cottages clustered near the church. Its sister hamlet of Sands has more to offer, including a stores, pub and bowling club. Here, too, is Farnham Golf Club.

But back to Seale where in 1788 at Hampton Lodge came the Derby winner of two years earlier, Noble, to stand at stud. A fee of two guineas and half a crown to the groom was fixed but Noble, in spite of his success at Epsom, was a failure at Seale.

In Elizabeth I's time a farmer from the hamlet went to the gallows for theft. Nicholas Grauntham appeared at Croydon Assizes on January 12, 1575, charged with the theft at Guildford of a purse, worth fourpence, which contained four shillings in money, a gold ring valued at a guinea, and a silver ring worth 16d.

Up on the ridge the Hog's Back Hotel was formerly a house on the site of a semaphore station, known as Poyle Hill, which was on the London to Plymouth line abandoned before completion in 1830.

St Lawrence's church is mostly Victorian on the site of a 13th century church built at the expense of Waverley Abbey. Among the memorials is one in the north transept to Edward Long, who perished in 1809 when the ship in which his regiment was sailing to Spain was sunk by a man-of-war in an accident. A school friend was responsible for erecting the tablet at Seale.

Between Seale and Elstead is Littleworth Cross where the architect Edwin Lutyens met the gardener Gertrude Jekyll for the first time. Lutyens designed a house called Squirrel Hill and it was in the garden of the famous rhododendron grower Harry Mangles that architect and gardener came together for a meeting that was to be the start of a great partnership. Across the road from that garden was, and still is, Littleworth Cross, a half-timbered house which may have been designed by Norman Shaw and contains some work by Lutyens.

Newark Priory, Send

Send Church

Send

Parish registers of the 18th century show just how strong was the military presence in Send. For 12 years from 1750 there was a camp on Send Heath and the records list many births, marriages and deaths of soldiers and their families. The men and their uniforms won the hearts of many a local girl. In 1759, 25 soldiers were married in the church of St Mary the Virgin; 14 went to the altar the following year; and 19 in 1761.

Three centuries earlier soldiers were involved in a skirmish in the area. On June 14, 1497, Cornish rebels marching on Kent reached Guildford and clashed with the outposts of the royal troops on the road to London. Old maps mark the spot where the road crossed the stream which joins the Wey near Send as St Thomas' Waterings.

The ruins of Newark Priory stand beside the river. It was founded by Ruald de Calva and his wife, Beatrice of Send, at the end of the 12th century, and was for the Augustinian order.

One of cricket's early giants. Edward Stevens, came from Send. Known as 'Lumpy' because of his size – or was it that he once ate an apple pie whole? – he was a member of the great Hambledon club towards the end of the 18th century. His last match was for England against Hampshire in 1789 when he was 54. Thirty years later, on September 7, 1819 he died and was buried in the churchyard at Walton-on-Thames where he had lived and worked as gardener to a great cricket supporter and twice Postmaster General, the Earl of Tankerville.

'Lumpy' was as good a bowler as there was and it was through his misfortune that a third stump was introduced. Until 1775 the wickets were of two stumps and many a straight delivery, having been missed by the batsman, went clean through the gap. It happened to 'Lumpy' on three occasions when he was bowling to the last man in a match between five of Hambledon and five of All England at the Artillery Ground in London. He got his man in the end and Hambledon won the game, but afterwards it was considerd 'not cricket' that a bowler should suffer so badly, and a middle stump was there and then brought in.

Shackleford

There is a lovely wooded lane in Shackleford where there are the remains of a lime kiln, long since disused. It has always fascinated me, but not until I read Gertrude Jekyll's explanation of the working of such a kiln did I have an understanding of its importance.

Miss Jekyll in *Old West Surrey* wrote that wagons brought chalk from a pit to the kilns which were 'built in steeply sloping ground by or near a roadside, where the loads of chalk could be drawn up to their top level. They are interesting wayside objects, and some of them that have been overgrown with brushwood, or that stand in what has become woodland, grown up during the 60 years or more that have passed since they were used, have an air of mystery that still brings back to me the thrill of fearful joy that they excited in my childish mind.'

The larger blocks of chalk, said Miss Jekyll, were built up inside the kiln (which was circular in plan and open at the top), in the form of a rough arch ... and the smaller pieces of chalk were filled in above. The space underneath was crammed with furze faggots, and a certain amount of burning converted the chalk into lime.

Shackleford has some interesting old cottages grouped around the village shop and there is an unusual wavy wall in one garden. Richard Wyatt, the son of a Sussex parson, was the squire more than three centuries ago. He lived at Hall Place which in Henry VIII's time had been the property of William de Shackleford. Hall Place was pulled down in 1797 and the land was added to nearby Peper Harow Park, but a new mansion was built in the 19th century and is now a preparatory school.

The church and school are apart from the village. St Mary's designed by the eminent architect Sir George Gilbert Scott in 1865 – among his other works is the Albert Memorial – stands proud on a crossroads opposite the war memorial in an area known as Norney and beloved of the authoress, Phyllis Nicholson, during the thirties and forties.

The narrow lane to Puttenham runs past Lydling where there is a farmhouse dating from about 1700 and where the Stovold family have farmed for centuries. The pond by the roadside is home to ducks and coots and moorhens, with occasional visits from swans and herons. A footpath through Lydling leads to Rodsall which was Redessolha in the Domesday Book. The Bishop of Bayeux held Rodsall at the time of the survey. Tovi held it before 1066 and 'could go with it where he would. Then it answered for five hides; now for nothing.' There was land for two ploughs, and there were three villagers and four cottagers with one plough. There were two acres of meadow and woodland with four pigs. The value before 1066 and at Domesday was 40s.

Shalford ✤

The Tillingbourne runs its course in this village just outside Guildford, and enters the Wey behind the church. Shalford suffers badly from being on the main road to Horsham, but there is enough charm off the beaten track to keep the visitor entertained.

It has recently basked in the glory of winning a section of the county's Best Kept Village competition; it was a deserved success.

Residents work hard to keep the place clean which is no easy task against the continual tide of traffic.

There are some pleasant walks around the village which was once an important landing stage when barges plied the Wey. Gunpowder from the Chilworth mills was brought the short distance to the river

Former gunpowder store at Broadford Bridge, Shalford

bank and transferred for the water-borne trip to the capital. Now, pleasure craft use the river which is navigable as far upstream as Godalming.

There were three mills in Shalford at the time of Domesday; there is one today. Shalford Mill, not too far from the church, was given to the National Trust in 1932. It was once the property of Major Arthur Godwin-Austen whose family is remembered on tablets in St Mary's church, a 1846 building on the site of the Domesday church. One of the Godwin-Austens explored and surveyed the north-west Himalayas.

The church end of the village is full of old houses and cottages, and the stocks are preserved outside the churchyard wall. It is a pleasant spot just a mile from the bustle of the county town.

Shamley Green 🍃

The Romans were in Shamley Green, which is not surprising in view of its proximity to the temple at Farley Heath. In 1900 a cinerary urn was discovered at nearby Blackheath, where today you can find good hospitality at the Villagers public house and a decent game of cricket next door; in the 1920s a coin was dug up when a well was being sunk at Green Lane Farm, and was identified as coming from Cyprus under Roman rule about AD 139; and as recently as 1970 a Romano-British burial urn was unearthed one foot below the surface when a post hole was being dug in Green Lane, and this contained cremated bones.

Shamley Green is a picturesque hamlet between Guildford and Cranleigh, with a charter for an annual fair granted by Oliver Cromwell to 'Shamble Lea'. Shops and houses are grouped around the green where cricket is played every summer weekend.

A tradition at Christ Church has it that when a funeral service is held a penny must be placed on the gatepost as the corpse is carried through the churchyard or a right of way will be established. The Congregationalists had a chapel built in 1836 but when interest declined the Strict Baptists moved in. Later, both denominations shared the building which eventually became so dilapidated that a new chapel was erected at the turn of the century.

Shepperton 🍃

Film studios have sent the name of Shepperton around the world, provided you read the small print as the credits roll. They have given the place a certain prosperity and brought a lot of famous names to the area. Shepperton is on the Thames and came into Surrey in the 1970s. The church of St Nicholas dominates the centre and was built with masonry from an earlier church which was demolished when the river undermined its foundations. A medieval rector was William Grocyn (1504-13) who was one of the first teachers of Greek at Oxford and a friend of Erasmus who occasionally visited him at the Rectory. Other guests at the Rectory have included Richard III, who was said to have stayed there before the battle of Bosworth Field, and the novelist George Eliot, who had connections elsewhere in Surrey, notably at Shottermill and Witley.

William Lindsay, MP, who became lord of the manor in the second half of the last century, is credited with achieving much for Shepperton. He transformed the lives of many residents who until his appearance on the scene were existing in one-room cottages. Lindsay also financed much of the building of the railway branch line from Twickenham which reached Shepperton and Sunbury in 1864.

In a district where one place merges with another, Shepperton's neighbour in one direction is Lower Halliford where, it is held, a weeping willow in the garden of the poet, Thomas Love Peacock, grew from a cutting sent to him from St Helena when Napoleon was exiled on that South Atlantic island.

Shere 🍃

Shere is the brightest jewel in the Tillingbourne valley's crown. The little river gurgles its way through the village where visitors and residents alike can sit on the banks and watch the ducks – descendants of those in Eric Parker's day. Since a bypass was built to the north in the 1960s, Shere has regained much of its calm. Overhanging buildings along the old A25 are no longer subjected to day and night traffic abuse. Visitors can look in peace.

The old ford, Shere

The village is the home of the Brays, a deep-rooted Surrey family whose members are remembered in St James's church. It was William Bray who completed the massive *History of Surrey* begun by the Rev. Owen Manning of Peper Harow, and whose volumes are much used by today's researchers. Manning died in 1801 and Bray, at the age of 65, took it upon himself to see that the work was finished. He visited every church and parish and will ever be in the debt of local historians. William Bray died in 1832 when aged 96.

The village rightly takes great pride in its appearance, and the church is no exception. There have always been parishioners keen and willing to look after the church, which was recorded in Domesday Book, and there is a portrait of one of them in the porch. Emma Diggins, who died in 1907, is shown unlocking the door, and the caption reads: 'Faithful servant of the church·'

Christine the Anchoress, the daughter of Edward the Carpenter, caused a stir in the village back in 1329. She wanted to carry chastity and Godly obedience to an extreme difficult to imagine in today's world. And she got her way when the Bishop of Winchester gave his permission for Christine to be incarcerated in a cell barely large enough to take her small frame. Her only contact with the outside world was a squint and an aperture through which food was passed. She remained in situ, as it were, for three years until she decided that she needed a break. The Bishop eventually consented and Christine emerged into the sunlight, but later she returned to her self-imposed captivity, there probably to die, although the outcome is not recorded.

Shere attracts painters which is not unnatural for a village that has been labelled the 'home of art' and where one house was, at different times, the home of three Royal Academicians – Gilbett, Holl, and Boehm. Smuggling and sheep stealing have also had a home in Shere, and so, too, has the cloth trade. It was Aubrey who said that the Old Parsonage House had been built upon 'woolsacks' or from the proceeds of the wool trade of the 17th century.

There is a brass in the church to Lord Audley whose son James was beheaded at Tower Hill for being a leader of the Cornish rebellion in 1497. James led his men through Shere on their way to Blackheath in Kent.

Shottermill ✣

Shottermill tends to be lumped on to Haslemere, but it deserves to be treated and looked at separately. Bordered by West Sussex and Hampshire, Shottermill tucks itself away under the hills of Hindhead and Blackdown. It has many picturesque corners, although one, the Ponds, is in West Sussex. The county boundary is the stream which runs through one of the parish's five mill sites, just below the London to Portsmouth railway line. To return to the ponds for a moment, they are two-tiered and were restored in 1955 as a memorial to the founders of the Haslemere Preservation Society, and are now owned by the National Trust.

The Trust, in fact, owns much land in Shottermill, whose ecclesiastical parish stretches up to the A3 at Hindhead and over the main road to the Hampshire border at Grayshott. Shottermill was in Frensham parish until the 1920s and was properly known as the tithing of Pitfold. Nowadays Pitfold is a quiet area off the A3 at the summit of the fearsomely steep Glen Lea, a narrow hill with a gradient of one in four which has tested cyclists for decades.

A reminder of Frensham control over the area is the property known as Frensham Hall close to a series of ponds from where the pioneering Surrey Trout Farm supplied the catch of many fishermen on rivers and streams throughout the land. Frensham Hall was the home of the well-known Baker family and by all accounts Edward Baker was none too popular back in the middle of the 19th century. One day as he rode home he discovered a trench had been dug across his path. And as he spurred his horse to jump the chasm a shot rang out and peppered his backside. Edward was determined that his 'exits and his entrances' would be carried out in safety so he built a lodge near the spot where the drive joined the highway to Hindhead. Another story about Edward concerned his pack of hounds. When his estate was being sold to pay off his creditors, he arranged for his huntsman, on hearing the hound pack's lot number called, to sound a blast on his horn and yell. The hounds disappeared as they had been trained to do.

Here at Shottermill, on the road down from St Stephen's church to the county boundary, lived George Eliot for a short time. She wrote much of *Middlemarch* here and the house in which she resided is easily identified by that name.

Smallfield &

The largely modern village of Smallfield owes its origins to the wars with France many centuries ago. It was in the reign of Edward III that the estate of Smallfield Place was given to John de Burstow by Lord Burghersh as an acknowledgement of the assistance he gave when his lordship was thrown from his horse in battle. The Bysshe family were later owners and Edward Bysshe extended the house. He was a bencher of Lincoln's Inn in the reign of James I. Bysshe's father had been MP for Bletchingley during the 1620s and in 1640, and Bysshe himself was a member for Gatton in Cromwell's first Parliament in 1654 and in Richard Cromwell's Parliament five years later.

Stanwell &

The name of this former Middlesex village is known to rose growers because in 1838 a hitherto unknown species was discovered in a local garden and given the name of Stanwell Perpetual.   Two of the oldest buildings in the Spelthorne borough are in Stanwell: St Mary's church and Lord Knyvett's School. The church at the end of the green has a beautiful spire which was added to the tower in the 14th century. There are monuments to Lord and Lady Knyvett who both died in 1622 and an arcade of eight seats, now used by the choir, which were thought to have been made for the monks of Chertsey Abbey and given to Stanwell in 1415.

Lord Knyvett's School was built in 1624 to educate 'male children'. Sir Thomas (late Lord) Knyvett was the man who arrested Guy Fawkes and he was granted the manor of Stanwell in 1603 and, 10 years later, the manor of Staines. One of the last owners of Stanwell Place before it was demolished was Sir John Gibson who was instrumental in the design of the Mulberry Harbours which played such an important part in the D-Day invasions of the Normandy coast nearly 50 years ago.

Stoke d'Abernon

Not too many people would put this village on the Mole on their honeymoon list, but William the Marshall did in 1189 and started a trend. William, or Guillaume le Marechal, and his bride, who was the heiress to the Earl of Pembroke, were offered Stoke Manor for the first honeymoon on record.

Stoke's church of St Mary the Virgin is the oldest in the county. It was built around 650AD but only the south wall of that period exists today. The restoration has been described as both 'merciless' and 'wicked'. Inside are the oldest monumental brasses in the country — those of the d'Abernon knights. A brass of a knight in chain armour dated 1277 is of Sir John d'Abernon and life size.

Sir John was Sheriff of Sussex and Surrey but in 1265 he got himself embroiled in a spot of bother which led to him having to pay out about £600. The trouble started when a William Hod of Normandy shipped to Portsmouth ten hogshead of woad. Robbers stole it and took it to Guildford. Hod set off in hot pursuit and seized back the woad and made it secure in Guildford Castle. But then events took a horrible twist as a counter-demand for the woad came from France and Sir John d'Abernon became involved, it seems, right up to his neck. There was a threat to burn down the castle, and even the town, and Hod took proceedings against Sir John and won after the under-sheriff had given in to the fresh demand. Sir John was ordered to hand over six score marks.

Stoke d'Abernon, whose church is one of only five on the banks of the Mole — Horley, Betchworth, Leatherhead and Cobham are the others — was *Stoche* in the Domesday Book and the rather grand appendage was added when the d'Abernon family were presented with the demesne. Elizabeth I stayed at the manor and the records show it was there she knighted Thomas Vincent, who was related to the d'Abernons.

Sunbury

The racecourse at Kempton Park means a steady flow of visitors to Sunbury. Kempton Park was enclosed in 1246 and kept stocked with deer until 1835. It has been used for horse racing for 95 years. St Mary's church, built in 1752 on the site of a 14th century building was designed by the clerk of works at Hampton Court. Sunbury Court, which is now used as a youth centre by the Salvation Army, was erected in 1770. To the west is the overgrown hamlet of Charlton with the delightful thatched roof 16th century Harrow inn.

Sutton Green

One house dominates this area near Guildford: Sutton Place. Built in the 1520s, it has been described as the best Tudor house in the south of England. Sir Richard Weston was granted the estate in 1521 after attending Henry VIII at the Field of the Cloth of Gold.

Weston, who built the house, was close to the king and remained so in spite of the fact that the monarch had Weston's son executed for suspicion of an affair with Anne Boleyn. That was in 1536, three years after Henry VIII visited Sutton Place. Weston's grandson, Sir Henry, became the heir to the estate and entertained Elizabeth I there for three days in 1591.

In 1613 the house and grounds came into the hands of another Sir Richard Weston who is remembered as the man who introduced canals to this country. He used a system he had seen in operation on the Continent to transform the river Wey between Guildford and Weybridge. Part of his inheritance was the village of West Clandon which he sold to Sir Richard Onslow in 1641. Weston the canal builder, who also brought the clover plant to this country, died in 1652 and his son John carried on his work and ensured that the Wey Navigation opened the following year.

The Wey was made navigable by Acts of Parliament in Charles II's reign. The work of building 12 locks and digging 10 miles of channel had cost Weston £15,000. In 1764 it was extended the four miles from Guildford to Godalming; 32 years later it was joined to the Basingstoke Canal; and in a further 20 years the Wey and Arun Junction Canal was linked to the system, although this latter section was forced to close by the growth of the railway in 1871. William Stevens became the approved wharfinger on the navigation in 1830 and Stevens' barges only ceased to trade commercially on the canal as recently as 1969, six years after Harry Stevens had given the Wey Navigation to the National Trust.

When the Weston family died out Sutton Place went through many changes until the beginning of this century when it was leased by the newspaper baron Lord Northcliffe. Then, in 1917, the Duke of Sutherland took it on. The American oil tycoon Paul Getty put Sutton Place on the tourist trail – Alan Whicker's television interview with the recluse is still recalled – but now it is owned by an American art collector and visiting is strictly controlled.

Tandridge

At the time of Domesday there was a Tandridge Hundred. Now, 900 years later, there is a Tandridge District Council. But the village of Tandridge in the hills near the eastern border with Kent is a quiet little place off the A25. The church dedicated to St Peter, is well worth visiting because at its western end there is one of Surrey's, if not England's, largest yew trees.

'Though quite hollow it is full of life.' records the *Victoria County History*. 'At about 4ft from the ground it spreads out into four great limbs, below which it has a girth of 32½ft. There is a great spread of branches, measuring 81ft from north to south.'

Manning and Bray, those other great Surrey historians, said the lower branches almost caressed the marble tomb of Mrs Scott, wife of the architect, Sir George Gilbert Scott. Today, the yew, heavily propped and fortified, does caress the tomb.

Sir Gilbert Scott, who died at nearby Rook's Nest, which is now a school, designed the north aisle of St Peter's in 1872. The church, which can be traced back to the 12th century, is on the site of pre-Christian worship and it is said that the foundations were built in such a way as not to damage the roots of the already formidable yew.

Tandridge Priory was at the foot of the Downs and was founded as a hospital, subsequently receiving Augustinian canons. Nothing except the fish ponds remains.

Tatsfield ⚜

By glancing at a map you can see so easily Tatsfield's position. Surrounded north-west and north-east by Greater London it fits into Surrey like a piece of a jigsaw puzzle. Its lofty heights are very much in the county, though, but look north and you see the London Borough of Bromley in the shape of Biggin Hill which was always in Kent when geography was being taught not too long ago.

Tatsfield vies for the title of the highest village in Surrey, and it is said that its inhabitants saw London burning in 1666. Its comparative remoteness even in modern times has led to food parcels having to be dropped by aeroplane when heavy snow blocked the roads. The blot on the landscape in recent times has been the construction of the M25. Now that it is open, the residents are faced with the vexed question of the siting of a service area, many feeling that it would prove an eyesore from the North Downs.

The 12th century church, whose dedication was not recorded, is 790ft above sea level. There is, as usual in these parts, a very old yew in the churchyard and a tombstone, to one Timothy Burgess who died in 1870, with the following doggerel:

'Once I stood as you do now,
And gaz'd o'er them as you do me;
And you will lie as I do now,
While others thus look down on thee.'

Thorpe ❧

'The village is picturesque and consists of a group of houses at the crossroads with others scattered along a winding road to the east.' That was the view of a writer in the first decade of this century, and it holds good today. Of course, there have been vast changes, like the arrival of the aeroplane at Heathrow, the construction of the M3 and M25 motorways, and the development of old gravel pits into a huge water and leisure park.

Thorpe appears to have survived these assaults on its privacy, and the stretch of Coldharbour Lane between the Red Lion and the village hall can be peacefully rural. The pub has been around at least since the start of the 18th century; the village hall for probably a hundred years longer. The latter, which has oak timbers, was a barn in the days when Thorpe was a farming community.

The village was mentioned in the Domesday Book as being held by Chertsey Abbey, but neither St Mary's church nor the mill on the tiny river Bourne was then in existence. St Mary's, which probably dates from the 1300s, stands attractively at the back of a small square off Coldharbour Lane. A 19th century worshipper was Capt. Hardy of Nelson fame who had a home in the village.

Great Fosters, an hotel close to Thorpe, has had a chequered history. It is reputed to have been built on the site of one of Henry VIII's hunting lodges and takes its name from Sir Robert Foster, Lord Chief Justice after the Restoration and staunch royalist. Roundhead soldiers made frequent searches of the house during the Civil War when Sir Robert was away with Charles I. And in the 18th century there were again searches when Sir Charles Orbey was the owner, as he was a suspected Jacobite.

In the reign of Good Queen Bess William Marten, a labourer, of Thorpe, was hanged after a jury at Guildford Sessions found him guilty of stealing seven sheep worth 12s. And Thomas Holloway of Egham also went to the gallows when he confessed to the burglary of John Hoult's house at Thorpe and stealing several pieces of linen, a cloak, a hat and a pair of stockings, together valued at £1 16s 4d.

Thursley

This heathy village on the northern slopes of Hindhead is fighting hard to survive. While it may be no bad thing to be bypassed by the busy London to Portsmouth road, only one of its three pubs remains and other services have diminished or disappeared.

But in days long ago Thursley was an important village. It was a staging post on the coach route between the capital and the coast before the long haul over the desolate summit of Hindhead, and was a centre of Surrey iron working.

Thursley has several times won best kept village competitions. Visitors are attracted by the peace and beauty of the countryside, and Thursley Bog is nationally known as an area of outstanding scientific interest. The churchyard has a stone which marks the grave of a man who was murdered more than two hundred years ago.

That stone is the single most sought out event in the history of the village. The grave to the north of the 950-year-old St Michael and

All Angels church tells the story of the foul deed on Hindhead in September 1786. The parish records state: 'September 27, 1786, was buried by the coroner's inquest a man unknown who was murdered on Hindhead on Sunday the 24th of September 1786 by Edward Lonegon, Michael Casey and James Marshall, three sailors who were afterwards hung in chains on Hindhead the 7th of April 1787.'

The unknown man in fact may have been a rich merchant named Hardman who had a love of the sea. A letter in a local newspaper in the 1930s purporting to have been written by a descendant of the victim, claimed that his wealth had still not been claimed. He was certainly unknown to his three attackers who befriended him on the Portsmouth road and shared his hospitality at the Red Lion at Thursley. But the trio, seeing their 'friend' was a man of means, hatched a plot which unfolded near the 895ft summit of Hindhead. There they murdered the unsuspecting traveller and threw his naked body over the rim of the Devil's Punch Bowl. A shepherd and his boy, who were in the Red Lion, came across the awful sight as they made their way over Hindhead, and the alarm was raised. The three killers were apprehended as they tried to sell the dead man's clothes, and were taken to the gaol at Guildford. Once tried and executed, their bodies were returned to Hindhead and hung in chains on the hill then known as Butterwedge.

The bodies, and subsequently skeletons, swung there on that breezy summit for more than three years before they crashed to the ground during a violent thunderstorm. The place became known as Gibbet Hill and is today marked by a granite cross.

A fascination with murder has ensured that the crime is never forgotten. Mysteriously, flowers have appeared on the grave at Thursley on the anniversary of the murder, and, it is claimed, men have died after moving a stone which marks the scene of the crime. The original memorial was replaced with one that, on its reverse, contained a warning that it should not be moved. But when the present road was cut in 1826 and subsequently widened the stone was moved and within a year one of the men involved in the work was dead at the age of 50.

Gibbet Hill and the Devil's Punch Bowl are traditionally linked to Hindhead although they are in the parish of Thursley. The Punch

Bowl is a deep hollow which can reflect the mood of the climate, and never more dramatically than on a damp day when mist spills over its rim as if the devil is boiling his cauldron. A few people continue to live in the Punch Bowl but the days when charcoal burners for the iron industry and broom makers worked side by side are gone. However, many of the old family names remain in the district and people are proud of their Punch Bowl roots.

Hammer ponds just off the A3 are a reminder of the iron industry. The furnace and forges were usually located in thick woods on quite small streams which were dammed to form the ponds. The water which was accumulated was diverted through an artificial channel to turn a wheel before rejoining the stream lower down.

Tilford 🌿

This is a village where cricket really is played on the green. And it has been that way for over one hundred years. The green is the focal point of Tilford and dotted around its perfect triangular shape are the church, school, institute and pub. Along two of its boundaries runs a river; the Till flowing in from the west and the Wey from the north to join in a meadow behind the Barley Mow, and run on to Elstead beneath sand cliffs known locally as the Rockies.

Tilford became a village with the building in 1867 of All Saints church. Until then it was a tithing of Farnham and sometimes called Tilford (or Tylford) Bridge or Tilford Green. The green, as waste of the Manor of Farnham, was handed over to the inhabitants for recreational use in 1835, but the cricket club was not formed until 1886 in spite of the earlier presence of the legendary player, William Beldham, who lived in a cottage on the edge of the green.

'Silver Billy' Beldham came to Tilford when he retired from playing cricket in 1822. He was then aged 55 and had played for Hambledon and on all three grounds made by Thomas Lord. He was for a time the landlord of the Barley Mow, which has been a pub for the best part of 200 years, but soon moved into Oak Cottage under the spread of Tilford's famous tree, which Cobbett, in 1822, said was by far the finest he had ever seen.

Alas, the tree is a sorry sight today, but it still stands and must be allowed to do so until it falls naturally. It has been there since the middle of the 17th century and not for a thousand years as legend would have it. Sadly, one of the three oaks on the green was lost in the Great Storm of October 1987, but has been replaced by a young tree grown from one of its acorns.

In Beldham's day the tree was as Cobbett saw it, and was a popular meeting place. It was sometimes known as Novel's Oak after a local resident. If it could speak what stories it would tell, including the one about how it was rescued from the woodman's axe by local people driving in nails to defy the Bishop of Winchester's instructions. The bishop, as Lord of the Manor, wanted the oak felled but had not reckoned with the people of Tilford.

Beldham, who was said to be the finest player of his age, lived to be 96. In the census of 1861, when he was in the last year of his life, he listed himself as 'old cricketer'. His home for 40 years still stands but with upstairs accommodation which was added in 1870, soon after the death of his second wife, Ann. The memory of Beldham lives on in the village, and especially in the Barley Mow where it is said his ghost has appeared on more than one occasion.

One of my favourite Tilford stories concerns the ice house close to Tilford House, which, when properly used, kept meat and fish fresh with the aid of blocks of ice cut from nearby Stockbridge Pond, and also served as a cooler to sober up the village drunks. The bobby, rather than walk them the three miles into Farnham, shut them in the darkened ice house for the night.

Titsey

To the north of Limpsfield, and separated by the M25 motorway, is Titsey Park, a heavily wooded area which was once the home of the Gresham family. Sir John Gresham pulled down the manor house in 1775 and rebuilt on the same site, and also removed the church, which was a matter of a few feet from the house, eventually to be rebuilt on its present site on the other side of the road. When the Greshams died out, the park was left to the Leveson-Gower family through marriage, and one of their number was responsible for discovering a Roman villa in the grounds in 1864.

Two Titsey labourers were hanged for breaking into the house of William Gresham in February 1575 and stealing £180. William Morley and Christopher Peryn were sentenced at Croydon Assizes 17 days after they committed the crime. Two yeomen from Titsey had gone to the gallows in the previous year for highway robbery. William Hankyn and Edward Rogers had been found guilty at Southwark Assizes of assaulting Richard Terrye in the highway at Godstone and stealing a cloak and dagger, together valued at 13s, and 2s in money.

Tongham

The village suffers from being in Aldershot's back pocket, and the industrial nature of the Hampshire town tends to rub off on its small neighbour. But for all that there are some pleasant corners in Tongham. The crossroads is an example. On one corner is the White Hart, a 50-year-old building on the site of a much earlier construction. Opposite is an oast house, now sadly not used for brewing purposes, but a reminder, nevertheless, that Tongham was once an important area in the brewing business. On another corner is a group of buildings with some 17th century work, and the whole has a nice feel about it:

Eric Parker wrote in 1908 that the entrance to Tongham from the Hog's Back was by way of 'The Avenue' which was 'pillared and canopied with lofty elms.' Now that road is called 'The Street' and the trees disappeared long before elms were felled by the Dutch disease.

Tongham was on the old Farnham to Guildford railway line and passengers used the station until 1937; goods up to 1960, the year before the line closed. In the Great War a building near the station was used as a munitions factory, and in 1939 it became billets for the RASC before being taken over by Tongham Ordnance Depot and being severely damaged by a big fire among imflammable stores.

The church is dedicated to St Paul and was consecrated in 1866. The first vicar and his wife had a son who became an Archbishop of York. The vicarage has a plaque which declares that Cyril Forster Garbett was Primate of England from 1947 to 1955.

Columns from Leptis Magna, Virginia Water

Virginia Water

The lakes and woodland walks to the west of the A30 are crowded at weekends. At times there are probably enough people around to reconstruct the Battle of Culloden. Culloden? Yes, Culloden, the famous Scottish plain east of Inverness where Bonnie Prince Charlie was routed in 1746. The English victor was the Duke of Cumberland who afterwards became Ranger of Windsor Park.

The Duke's deputy was Thomas Sandby, an outstanding architect and landscape gardener, and between them they devised a scheme to drain a large area of marshy ground in the park. Sandby, with the assistance of his brother, Paul, settled on the idea of a vast lake, and today's visitors can thank these 18th century men for their expertise. The lake was enlarged to its present area of around 120 acres later in that century. George IV had a scaled down frigate built for the lake. It was still in use in Queen Victoria's reign and was brought out at her request. A lieutenant and six sailors sailed it along the lake and fired a royal salute from its cannon.

It is perhaps ironic that the victor of Culloden (who was afterwards known as 'Butcher' Cumberland) should have created such beautiful landscape so close to the possible site of even greater butchery in AD60 - that of the final battle between the Roman 14th Legion and Queen Boudicca's army of Britons in rebellion. There are sound reasons (see *London Archaeologist* Autumn 1983 issue) for believing the site to have been between Callow Hill and Knowl Hill - certainly it fulfils Tacitus' description of the Roman position being approached by a narrow defile with a wood behind and a plain in front.

A little to the west are the genuine remains of a fine Roman building recovered from Leptis Magna near Tripoli in North Africa. They were brought to England and presented to the Prince Regent in 1816. A proposal to use them for the portico of the British Museum never materialised and they were set up here as a landscape ornament in 1826.

The village of Virginia Water, which has a station, appears to be little more than a dormitory for London. There are many large houses, and the world famous Wentworth golf club has attracted millionaire neighbours.

Surrey runs into Berkshire about here – indeed much of the woodland area about the lake is in the Royal County – but the A30 continues to run through Surrey on its way towards the capital, and there are more public gardens and walks before Egham and the Thames are reached.

Walton-on-the-Hill

There is a 12th century lead font in St Peter's church, and it is believed to be the oldest in the country. It is the only one in the county and there are just 30 in England. It has a frieze of foliage around its top and its bottom, and there are eight figures, seated, in relief under arches. Walton-on-the-Hill is separated from its neighbour, Headley, by the M25 on the stretch between Wisley and Reigate. It has a world famous golf course, Walton Heath, which in 1981 was the venue for the Ryder Cup tournament.

Lutyens and Jekyll were there earlier this century, and much earlier the Romans left their mark. A Romano-British villa at Sandilands Road was excavated in 1948 and contained 13 rooms. It was built in the 1st century AD. and after being unused for 50 years was renovated and remained in use until around the year 400 AD when it was destroyed.

Wanborough

It seems improbable now that a tiny collection of buildings just north of the Hog's Back was often, a century ago, the centre of government. When Gladstone was prime minister, his parliamentary private secretary was the tenant of Wanborough Manor, and the Liberal leader was a frequent visitor. Cabinet meetings were held there. Queen Victoria came to stay as the guest of Sir Algernon West. Gladstone, in fact, wrote his farewell speech at Wanborough. Asquith became a sub-tenant of the manor at the beginning of the 20th century, and two of his daughters are buried in the churchyard of St Bartholomew's next door.

The church is the second smallest in the county – it measures 45 ft by 18 ft – and is 13th century on the site of a Domesday building. When it fell into disrepair in the 1600s it became a carpenter's shop, but as restoration work to Puttenham church became necessary, St Bartholomew's was itself restored and reopened in June 1861.

Wanborough was an important farm in the days of Waverley Abbey. About 800 acres were bought in 1130 from a nephew of Queen Adeliza, and the abbots had a large fish pond just north of the grange. When the abbey was dissolved in 1536 one of the monks, John Parker, went as curate at Wanborough.

West, the PPS to Gladstone, was a director of the London and South Eastern Railway, and was responsible for having a station sited close to Wanborough so that his important guests might arrive by train. The station is in fact on the edge of Normandy village and was opened in September 1891. The line, which links Reading and Gatwick via Guildford was opened in 1847. Nearby is the curiously named Christmas Pie hamlet whose name has been a puzzle for generations. Seventeenth century maps list a Christmas Farm, and a correspondent to the *Surrey Advertiser* 30 years ago stated there was at one time a Pie Farm. Another story runs that there was a farmer named Christmas – a common enough West Surrey name – who had a large family but nothing to eat at the festive season. He went into the woods and bagged some rabbits which his wife cooked into a pie, and the name was coined.

Warlingham 🦌

A gardener was digging his plot one spring day in 1909 when his spade unearthed some pieces of pottery. Further, careful digging uncovered many more fragments and some burnt bones. The site was about 200ft north of the Westerham road between the village and the Hare and Hounds pub and caused much excitement.

An expert was called in and built up the outline of a cinerary urn 10in in diameter, and dated it to the first century. The bones were thought to be that of a child and burnt, presumably, in the urn.

Warlingham has the Greater London boundary to its north and is very much commuter country with a station close by. Here, a century and more ago, young boys whipped the apple trees in spring in an attempt to make them bear more fruit.

All Saints church is restored 13th century and is reputed to be where the Edward VI-authorised prayer book was first used, when Archbishop Cranmer attended a service. There are some picturesque listed buildings near the green, including the White Lion, which is 18th century, and the almshouses and the vicarage which were both built in 1663.

Waverley 🦌

There never has been a village of Waverley in Surrey but this area near Farnham has contributed to the beauty of many places in the county. The first Cistercian abbey in England was built here beside the Wey in 1128 and when it was dissolved in 1536 its stones were used for buildings far and wide. Many of the bridges in the district were undoubtedly built by Waverley monks. The abbey ruins can be seen from the Farnham to Godalming road, and have recently been reopened to the public.

The road twists violently at Waverley as it crosses the river at the spot where there was a mill, whose miller in the 1570s, Barnard Rowe, was sentenced to hang for theft. He appeared at Croydon Sessions in January 1576 charged with stealing silver, gilt hooks, silver pins, a harness girdle, a silver buckle, five pieces of gold, a sheet, two handkerchiefs and a cassock, together valued at £5 4s 8d, from a widow of Aldershot, Catherine Lague. Rowe's two accomplices, Richard Fowkes, a miller, and Hugh Tarrant, a husbandman, also of Waverley, were 'at large' when he went to the gallows.

Just across the road from the mill site is Stella Cottage, named after Esther Johnson, beloved of Jonathon Swift, whom he called Stella. Swift came to the area as secretary to Sir William Temple, a noted diplomat, who lived in Moor Park, a mansion still standing, which was built in 1630. Swift wrote *Tale of a Tub* there, and undoubtedly meditated in the area around Mother Ludlam's Cave. The legend of Mother Ludlam the white witch of Waverley, has been handed down to children through the ages. Her cave is tatty now, tattier no doubt than when Cobbett wrote in 1825: 'Alas it is no longer the enchanting place that I knew it. The semi-circular palings are gone; the basins to catch the never-ceasing little streams are gone, the iron cups, fastened by chains for people to drink out of, are gone; the pavement all broken to pieces; the seats for people to sit on, on both sides of the cave, torn up and gone; the stream that ran down through a clean paved channel, now making a dirty gutter; and the ground opposite, which was a grove chiefly of laurels, intersected by closely mown grass walks, now become a poor ragged-looking alder coppice.'

Westcott ⚜️

The man who gave us the *Principle of Population* was born in Westcott. Thomas Malthus, a clergyman and economist, contended that as population increased faster than the means of subsistence, its growth could only be checked by normal restraint or by disease and war. Malthus (1766-1832) was born at The Rookery to the south of Coast Hill on the west side of the village. His father, David, bought the house with its extensive grounds which he landscaped by using the Pippbrook stream to the full.

There was a mill at The Rookery and another at Westcott. In fact, the tiny Pippbrook, which rises on the northern slopes of Leith Hill and flows only a matter of a few miles to join the Mole, at one time supplied the water for six mills.

Westcott became an ecclesiastical parish, separate from Dorking, in 1852 when the Sir Gilbert Scott-designed Holy Trinity church opened. The church and burial ground occupy a fine site above the A25 and are approached through a lych gate which was provided by public subscription in 1890. The village is attractive in spite of the rush of traffic, with a green on which there is a dovecote. Nearby is a public house whose name has recently been restored to that of The Cricketers after a short period as, of all things, The Wizard.

South of the village, in Squire's Wood, there was in times past a watering hole by the name of Mag's Well. It was said to be a medicinal spring and children bathed in it.

West Humble

The A24 winds around the western side of Box Hill which has been a most favoured beauty spot in the county for generations. Daniel Defoe observed that an 'abundance of gentlemen and ladies from Epsom (came) to take the air and walk in the box woods'. Nowadays thousands of day trippers have turned Box Hill into a place to avoid at peak periods. Off-peak, though, it is a good place to be, to wander over the chalky acres and admire the view south across the valley of the Mole as the river meanders through meadows from its source in Sussex.

At West Humble is the beautiful Burford Bridge Hotel where, when it was known as the Fox and Hounds, Nelson spent his last night ashore before the Battle of Trafalgar, and farewelled Lady Hamilton. The poet Keats was also a guest at the inn and claimed that a walk on Box Hill by moonlight gave him inspiration for part of *Endymion*.

Up on Box Hill there is a curious memorial which has fascinated visitors for years. It is the burial place of an eccentric from Dorking, Major Peter Labelliere, an 18th century Marines officer, who demanded that in his final resting position he be upside down so that 'as the world was turned topsy turvy he might come right at last'. The Mad Major had his way, or at least it is presumed he had his way, and millions of people have had a chuckle at his expense.

Down on the valley floor in West Humble a chapel was built because of the difficulty in getting across the Mole to the nearest parish church. In an early 19th century publication, *The Promenade round Dorking*, it is recorded that the Mole had rapid currents and such depth that a boat was upset and several gentlemen drowned. The river dries up and goes underground in very hot spells which gives credence to the claim of Celia Fiennes that 'just about Dorken and Leatherhead it sinkes away in many places which they call swallow holes'.

Weybourne

A ribbon development village north-west of Farnham on the road to Aldershot. John Henry Knight, the inventor and motoring pioneer, was born at Weybourne House in 1847 and removed to Barfield at nearby Runfold in 1888. Knight was a man clearly ahead of his time, whether it be in the motoring field or in photography, and there is a fascinating collection of examples of his work in the district which periodically surfaces. His birthplace, Weybourne House, was believed to have been built in 1729 by Peter Coldham who was at one time the owner of Waverley Abbey near Farnham. Farnham council purchased the property in 1947.

Weybourne's two pubs are old established hostelries. The Elm Tree stands near the crossroads and presumably takes it name from a large elm tree that stood proudly by the roadside. The Running Stream is very close to the Hampshire border and was the local of a well-known Farnham character who was known to all as the rag and bone man. His horse and cart were daily to be seen outside the Running Stream; indeed it was suggested, probably unfairly, that it was the only pub in the district which extended the man a welcome.

Whiteley Village

When William Whiteley came south from his native Yorkshire in 1851 he could not have realised what effect that would have in the 20th century. Whiteley, who died in 1907, left one million pounds which was to be used to build a retirement village, and today that community thrives.

Whiteley was born in 1831 and when he was 20 he journeyed down to London to view the Great Exhibition. He liked the capital enough to want to stay and ten years later opened a small shop in Westbourne Grove. That business grew into Whiteley's Store in Bayswater and made William Whiteley a millionaire.

The person to whom Whiteley had taken his idea, the Bishop of London, Dr Winnington-Ingram, became the first chairman of the trustees, and was joined by the philanthropist's two sons. Whiteley stipulated that the village was to be west of London, no more than ten miles from Charing Cross, and not to be sited on clay soil. They were instructions that could not be met mainly because of the nature of the land around the capital, and eventually a site was settled on 17 miles out on the Burhill Estate of Viscount Iveagh. It was land where pines and rhododendrons grew in profusion and the soil was typically Surrey: sandy.

Six architects were invited to submit designs and Robert Frank Atkinson was commissioned to proceed with his vision of an octagonal community with a memorial to Whiteley as the centrepiece. Five other architects then joined Atkinson in designing the buildings. Work started shortly before the Great War and by Armistice Day a few people had moved in.

The church of St Mark was dedicated by the Bishop of Winchester on the saint's day, April 25, in 1918, and by the time King George V and Queen Mary visited the village in 1920 to open the social centre 284 people were in residence.

Whiteley Village today nestles in the comfortable and well-heeled hinterland of Weybridge and Esher, and is worth a visit if only to see what is thought to be a unique idea in community living.

Windlesham 🌿

Aubrey enthused over this place on the western edge of Chobham Common when he was on his walkabout through the county. He fastened on to the reputation for growing bog-myrtle, and wrote: 'In this parish, at Light-Water-Moor, grows great store of a plant, about a foot and a half high, called by the inhabitants Gole, but the true name is Gale; it has a very grateful smell, like a mixture of bays and myrtle, and in Latin is called *Myrtus Brabantica;* it grows also in several places of this healthy country, and is used to be put in their chests among their linnen.'

The church of St John the Baptist went up in 1680 four years after its predecessor had been struck by lightning. In the churchyard there is a gravestone with the curious epitaph:

'She was, but words are wanting to say 'What',
Thinking what a wife should be, and she was 'That'.'

The men from Windlesham who were killed in the Great War are remembered by a Celtic cross which was unveiled by Hermione Lady Ellenborough of Windlesham Court in 1920. They would have remembered the village as it was described by Eric Parker: ... 'straggles over a dozen short crooked roads – an oasis among parallelograms.'

Wisley

Wisley means the Royal Horticultural Society gardens. Thousands of visitors walk around the lovely acres every year. The gardens came into the possession of the RHS following the death of the society's treasurer, Mr G.F. Wilson, who owned 60 acres of shrubs and flowers at Wisley. They were purchased by Sir Thomas Hanbury who gave them to the RHS which moved from Kew in 1904. The area is almost treble what it was in Mr Wilson's day when Eric Parker wrote that 'experiment and officialdom have settled heavily on its sandy soil, and the wilder charm of the old pleasance has left it.' Parker observed that in Mr Wilson's day the gardens were a delight to many hundreds of visitors. Wisley has clearly improved with age.

There was uproar in 1869 when the locals got to hear of a proposal to enclose 362 acres of Wisley Common, and the plan was dropped. Since then, development has eroded much of the countryside but Bolder Mere remains. It is a 10-acre shallow lake, currently favoured by windsurfers, and previously beloved of customers of the Hut Hotel which once stood beside the Portsmouth Road. Sadly, that hostelry was demolished in the name of progress, or at least a faster stretch of A3, just as the Half Moon at Thursley disappeared long before that section of the same trunk road was transformed into a dual carriageway.

The village of Wisley is a mile or so from the Gardens and is very rural. The lane which serves as the main street wanders between houses, crosses quite a wide stretch of the Wey and bends past the little Norman church. Beside the church, which has no dedication, is a delightful old farmhouse and the two taken together epitomise the timelessness of the area.

Witley 🌿

Traffic races through the village on its way to Sussex and the coast which is no way to see its beauty and its charm. Witley has been a thriving place for a long time. Its church was recorded in Domesday Book. The court of Edward I met at Witley on at least one occasion – for a few days in June 1305.

The parish once was in four tithings: Milford and Mousehill; Ley or Lea which included Wheeler Street; Stoatley; and Birtley which included Witley Street and Witley Park. The modern parish of Witley encompasses the villages of Milford, Wormley and Brook and district. A railway station means the area is home for commuters who can enjoy fast travel to London while living among beautiful undulating south-west Surrey pineland.

Witley Park, which is enclosed by six miles of wall, was once known as Lea Park and was where Cobbett often rested overnight. The wall – 'the finest in England' was how one newspaper report described it in 1905 – cost £37,000 to build and enclosed 1400 acres of land. Mr Whitaker Wright, a financier built the mansion at a cost of £840,000 at the turn of the century and, being the amateur landscaper that he was, spent another half-million on laying it out. This included a glass-roofed ballroom under a lake. There was even a scheme to turn Lea Park into a racing centre to rival Ascot and Epsom, but Whitaker Wright's tenure ended abruptly when he committed suicide in 1904 after a prison sentence for fraud.

Social troubles in 1549 led to riots in Witley. The 'general rebellion' in these parts was largely against the enclosing of lands. One of those who rebelled may have been John Porter, a farmer, of Witley. Twenty-three years later he strangled his wife Margery as she lay asleep, and a jury at Southwark Assizes on February 26, 1673, found him guilty and he was sentenced to death by hanging.

At the top of Church Lane in the early part of the 19th century there was a semaphore station for relaying messages between the Admiralty in London and ships off Portsmouth. The stations either side of Bannicle, as Witley's was known, were at Pewley in Guildford, and Haste Hill at Haslemere. Families of the men worshipped at All Saints church which with its attendant group of cottages comprises one of the most pleasant corners in the county. Step

Cottage, close to the church, has been photographed so often it must be known around the world.

Woldingham

A decade ago a plan by the Government to build a rail link to the much talked about Channel Tunnel raised the hackles of the local people. The plan was to use land at Marden Park for the terminus, but the public outcry was such that the idea was abandoned. Back in 1836 there was a similar outpouring of concern over plans to drive the railway through the area. The pre-Victorian worthies won that day and their successors wrangled for almost 50 years before losing out as the railway network took a hold. The Croydon and East Grinstead line opened in 1884 and long tunnel took it under Woldingham. A garden village was built near the station during the First World War, and first saw life as an army camp.

St Agatha's church, first mentioned in 1270, is the smallest in the county at 30ft 3in by 20ft 2in. And at 797ft above sea level it is the third highest old parish church in Surrey, behind those at Coldharbour and Abinger. The village's other church, St Paul's, was built in 1905.

Wonersh

Wonersh Blue was famous in Elizabethan times. No, it wasn't cheese but cloth. This was a cloth-making centre and the clothiers dyed their garments with woad. The trade in blue cloth from Wonersh was particularly brisk in the Canary Islands, but eventually greed got the better of the manufacturers whose dishonesty in stretching their webs was their downfall. By the 17th century cloth-making had dwindled to next to nothing in the district.

The pub in the centre of the village is called the Grantley Arms after the family who owned the big house in Wonersh Park. Sir Fletcher Norton who became the first Baron Grantley, was Speaker of the House of Commons from 1769 to 1782. His grandson,

George, had an unhappy marriage and kidnapped his children, holding them hostage at Wonersh Park. His wife Caroline's fight to get them back eventually led to the Custody of Infants Bill becoming law in 1839.

The mansion was demolished in the 1930s and some land that had been enclosed was returned to the people as a village green. The church of St John the Baptist is close by and was rebuilt in 1796 to, according to one legend, the design of Lord Grantley's butler after fire had greatly damaged it three years earlier. The church, which once had fine box pews and a triple decker pulpit, was restored at the beginning of the 20th century.

Wormley

This scattered area between Witley and Chiddingfold has at its heart King Edward's School which commands attention on the crest of the hill on the main road. The school came to Surrey in 1867 to cater for destitute boys who, recorded the *Victoria County History*, 'have never been committed of crime and who are trained for the army, navy or industrial life'. It had been founded in London in 1552. Today, King Edward's takes girls as well and has an outstanding academic and sporting name, as befits an establishment which had an Olympic Games representative, the Rev. A.C.B. Bellerby, as headmaster from 1926 to 1961. During the war Mr Bellerby, his staff and pupils were installed in the Institute at nearby Hambledon while King Edward's was taken over by the Admiralty which developed naval radar there – almost a century and a half after the Admiralty relied on a semaphore station at Bannicle in neighbouring Witley to get its messages to the ships off Spithead.

The wartime radar work at King Edward's was used in the Battle of the Atlantic, and Wormley continues to have a link with the sea through the presence of the Institute of Oceanographic Science whose headquarters are situated close to the school.

Worplesdon

In the days of the semaphore system of sending messages via the Admiralty in London and the ships in the Channel, Worplesdon was one of the stations on the ill-fated line to Plymouth. The semaphore building was a tower adjacent to the church and a contemporary print displays a peaceful scene with sheep grazing outside the churchyard wall. Worplesdon Glebe Station was demolished in 1851, 20 years after the line was abandoned. The branch to Plymouth had begun in 1825 from Chatley Heath on Ockham Common, where there was a station on the line to Portsmouth. Worplesdon and Poyle Hill (Hog's Back) were the Surrey stations before the messages entered Hampshire.

St Mary's church was described at the turn of the century as being on the 'summit of a gentle hill in a churchyard of considerable beauty'. Even in the built-up eighties, the area of the church retains that quality. Worplesdon is a parish of contrasts and far enough removed from Guildford to have a peaceful air about it.

Whitmoor Common has been claimed as the place of Wibbandun where Caeulin, King of the West Saxons, met Ethelbert, King of Kent, in battle in AD568. And at Slyfield Green, which is now part of industrial Guildford, Aubrey recorded that there had been an attempt to find coal. The would-be miner was Rev. Giles Thornborough, rector of St Nicolas and Trinity, Guildford, who in 1671 found a type of stony coal when grubbing the roots of an old oak tree. Aubrey wrote that Thornborough dug to a depth of about 150ft and found a rocky coal but after spending £400 the pit fell in.

A Worplesdon man who was more successful was Benjamin Martin who began life as a plough boy and ended it as an optician in Fleet Street where he died in 1782 aged 77. Martin learned the three Rs and taught them in Guildford before studying mathematics and astronomy and travelling the country.

The area in the parish called Jacobs Well has given rise to much speculation about its origins. According to the curator of Guildford Museum the name first appeared on the Worplesdon tithe map of 1839. Although there are wells in the area there is, as yet, no evidence of a local inhabitant called Jacob who might have lent his name to the place.

Wotton 🦜

This is Evelyn country. The famous diarist, John Evelyn, was born at Wotton House and is buried in the church of St John the Evangelist on the other side of the A25. A descendant, Patrick, was the county's high sheriff in 1982. Wotton House, which came into the Evelyn family in 1579 when John's grandfather, George, bought it. It may become an hotel.

The church is down a lane and looks out over the North Downs. It is the family burial place of the Evelyns, and, said John, was where he received the rudiments of his education. 'I was not initiated into any rudiments till I was four years of age, and then one Frier taught us at the church porch of Wotton'.

A church at Wotton is not mentioned in Domesday Book although it has been suggested that part of it is early Norman. Wotton Hundred at the time of the survey stretched from Abinger Hammer in the west to Betchworth in the east, and Wotton, which had been held by Harold, was then held by Oswald. There was a mill recorded and this seems certain to have been at Friday Street, a mile or two south and now a favourite haunt of ramblers.

Wrecclesham

If there was a title awarded to the best beer-drinking village in Surrey then Wrecclesham, on performances admittedly more past than present, would surely win. As Alice Holt Forest receded hop-bines were planted and the area outside Farnham became a vast garden for the numerous ale houses and breweries. Eighty years ago the situation so disgusted an Australian who had come to live in Farnham that he wrote to a Liberal publication, *The Speaker*, as follows: 'There is one licence to every 126 inhabitants (in Farnham), with the result that during the eight months I have been in the district I have seen more drunk people than during the previous 12 years in Adelaide, with a population more than ten times as large. It is very necessary that something be done to lessen the evil, which is even worse in the surrounding villages. About two miles from here is a village called Wreekelsham (sic), with a population of 600, and in its main street there are five licensed houses within 200 yards, besides another in a side street, and several grocer's licences. On Monday afternoons the whole village is drunk, and one has to drive through it very carefully.' Tut tut. The local newspaper also published the letter and with one eye on its circulation figures defended its readers. The allegation was a 'statement so foolish as not to be worthy of contradiction'.

There are three pubs now in the main street and one, The Cricketers, is striving to restore some of the glory it knew back in the late 18th and early 19th centuries when it was 'home' to two of the

159

greatest players of the noble game in Georgian times. William 'Silver Billy' Beldham and 'Honest' John Wells were brothers-in-law and used The Cricketers as their local. Beldham's brother John was at one time the landlord and for many years the hostelry bore the signs: 'Rendezvous of those great cricketers, Beldham and Wells' and 'Village's best beer as drunk by those famous men, Beldham and Wells.' Beldham, the farmer son of a yeoman farmer, was born in 1766 in what is now Old Yew Tree Cottage in Wrecclesham. He joined the famous Hambledon club in 1887 and was a giant at the game for 40 years. A hoax played on the 19th century cricket statistician, Arthur Haygarth, has led to the myth that Beldham fathered something approaching 39 children, but extensive research by this author has established that from two marriages (his first wife died soon after giving birth to her first child) he was the father of nine, and from the line through the son he named William there are descendants living in Dorset and Kent who came together in 1982 when Beldham was remembered as a founder of Farnham Cricket Club 200 years earlier.

Because of the proximity of the forest, Wrecclesham's inhabitants were often referred to as 'outlaws'. They were said to be a lawless breed. It would have been a wild place at the time of Domesday when its two mills were probably among the six recorded as being in the Farnham Hundred. The mills were not named in the 1086 survey; Wrecclesham's were Willey, now a private house, and Weydon, or Le Medmulle, whose sluices can be detected beside Farnham bypass.

Willey stands beside the A31 and close to the county boundary. The water meadows on the banks of the Wey contrast nicely with the trees of Alice Holt Forest. This area is known as Runwick and lanes climb northwards into Hampshire. Wrecclesham is well known for its blue gault clay, and the pottery on high ground behind the Royal Oak has been in existence since 1873. It was founded by Absolam Harris, who had worked clay at Charles Hill, Tilford, and was continued by his son, William, then grandsons Reg and Arthur, and, until his death in 1983, great grandson Reg. Six years ago the family said there was a deposit of blue clay at the pottery which could last for 40 years.

Surrey lane

Bibliography

Books on Surrey are numerous, but many are out of print and hard to obtain. My collection has been put together through years of ferreting in secondhand shops. Three titles, *History of Surrey* by H.E. Malden, first published in 1900, *Highways and Byways in Surrey* by Eric Parker, written in 1908, and *Surrey* (the Buildings of England series) by Ian Nairn and Nikolaus Pevsner, who died within a few days of one another in 1984, are required reading by any student of the county. Much earlier came the Manning and Bray volumes, Brayley's history, the *Victoria County History* series and Aubrey's writings, which are in main libraries. Many village history societies and local authorities have published material which is available in the local studies library in Guildford where John Janaway and his staff offered me all the help I required in my researches. Much of my material has come from notes collected over the years, and from the files of the *Surrey Advertiser* and the *Farnham Herald* newspapers.

Index